Joe & Tammy —

Blessings for your
journey —

Dan

Required reading for anyone committed to living, loving, and leading with greater mastery. One of the few books providing guidance for when things come apart. No one I know traverses this terrain as masterfully. If you have faith and courage, you will emerge with new-found powers of creativity, vitality, character and leadership.

BOB ANDERSON, founder, Soul Works Inc.

Dan Holden brings an articulate, practical mind and the heart of a mystical poet and teacher to our darkest moments of alienation and doubt. I am grateful for his insight and ferocious commitment to explore a common human experience we too often keep hidden. It is inspiring to hear from someone who has been cut by the same stone and has transformed the wound into renewed wonder.

MIKA AMURU, PH.D., author of *Reporting from the Wilderness: A Guide for Guides*

*Lost Between Lives* skillfully and compassionately brings bright new light to a very rich and prevalent theme for the archetypal Spiritual Seeker. Dan Holden's vibrant style of discourse and storytelling lends itself brilliantly to his heartfelt message of encouragement and perseverance.

KEITH VARNUM, author of *Inner Coach, Outer Power*

# LOST

### between

# LIVES

# Guest House

*This being human is a guest house*
*Every morning a new arrival.*
*A joy, a depression, a meanness.*
*Some momentary awareness comes*
*as an unexpected visitor.*
*Welcome and entertain them all!*
*Even if they're a crowd of sorrows,*
*Who violently sweep your house*
*empty of it's furniture,*
*Still, treat each guest honorably.*
*He may be clearing you out*
*for some new delight.*

—Rumi (A.D. 1207–1273)

# LOST
## between
# LIVES

Finding *Your* Light
When the World Goes Dark

## DANIEL HOLDEN

WingFire
PRESS

LOST BETWEEN LIVES
Finding *Your* Light When the World Goes Dark

For permission requests, contact:

Wingfire Press
1028 Boulevard, #299
West Hartford, CT 06119-1801

www.wingfirepress.com
info@www.wingfirepress.com

Printed in the United States of America

Daniel Holden, Lost Between Lives:

LCCN   20041001  67

ISBN 0 - 9747186 - 3 -7

PCIP
1. Leadership    2. Conduct of Life   3. Encouragement  I Title
BF637. L4H65 2004  158'.4
                    QBI33 - 1754

Book consultant: Ellen Reid
Cover photograph: Douglas Fogelson
Book design: Dotti Albertine
Author photograph: Bob Hankins

When things are going great, there's no felt need to change. What if your life, or God, for reasons unknown to you, turns everything upside down to get your attention? Events that bring change—even change that ultimately proves to be for our benefit—seldom come as invited house guests! Yet, their unexpected arrival is always perfectly timed for our unfolding if we can greet them.

Dan Holden doesn't say anyone needs to change anything. Unless, of course, your life seems to have fallen apart, God appears to have abandoned you, and the best bed partner you can get at night is depression. Face it: when you're in deep enough there's no getting out. Your own strength will not save you now. You need something or someone to break in.

But how do you do that when you're wandering around lost in your own life? That's what Dan addresses in clear, concise, practical terms. From the vantage point of one who's made the journey, he points out the pathways and pitfalls along the way. And, when there are shortcuts to get through it all, Dan shows you how to find them. The power of this book is in the way he opens the whole process from the wreckage to the resurrection of your life.

Dan is a trailblazer with a radically different approach: real time, non religious partnership with Spirit for real people. Each of us has this switch within; few know how to turn it on. Dan shows you how.

This book is not about weakness, drama and tragedy. It is a road map to finding opportunities for building strength beyond what you might have ever imagined for yourself. It is a specific and practical guide to finding inner allies, spirit guidance, and methods for accessing wisdom and resources you didn't know you had. Best of all, it's a book that shows you how to shine light into the depths and darkness of your very being when you need it the most and emerge stronger, more resilient and whole.

## Acknowledgements

A great many people played active roles in bringing this book to fruition. John Davis and, later, John Bermon were instrumental in helping me see that the aspects of me I despise are significant aspects of who I am that actually need to be celebrated and shouted from the roof tops! It is, after all, these deeper qualities of the soul that leak to the surface during times of great change. Why not befriend them early and strike up a conversation?

A special thanks goes to Bob Anderson, a close friend and advisor, who continues to help me and many other leaders find our true voice when so many other voices cry for our attention. Your encouragement over the years, Bob, has opened my heart to who I am and what I am here to do. And your support of this work has been invaluable. When you referred to what I wanted to do as making "inner road maps for real people in crisis," I knew what I wanted to write about. Up until that moment I had been writing about something important to me. Instantly, I knew I was a guide recording the inner landscape for a much larger community of people who were passing through a place called "Lost." One huge, terrifying leap! As vital as your encouragement has been, the tears welling up in my eyes now confirm that your friendship and love matter more to me.

To Doug Olsen who called me one night and read an exquisite poem over the phone. When I exclaimed,"What a beautiful piece . . . can you fax it to me?" you reminded me, "You idiot, you wrote this poem yourself and gave it to me last year!" I began looking for an editor the next day.

Carl Nord and Skip Jordan are friends as well as corporate leaders who read early chapters of the book and reminded me (with your tears and comments) that I was not crazy. This personal journey was not mine alone but needed to be shared with many others who experienced the same kinds of trauma in the place called, "Lost."

The living room in Barbara Riley's home where the Spirit Weavers meet has been a secret retreat space for many of us who were hungry for nourishing dialogue about practical spirituality. Good food, great music, intimate check-ins that go on not quite long enough have been the emotional soil in which the ideas, form and focus of this book incubated. Every time we meet you quietly ask, "How's the book coming?" Writing can be a lonely sport; your inquiry kept me connected and accountable. A special thanks to each and every one of you.

To my Thursday night FA family who model a fierce yet compassionate kind of loving that opens me to a life worth living—my own—and to a way of living it well in the face of unresolved struggle and suffering. This short sentence cannot capture the depth of my gratitude to your individual and collective courage, fortitude, and passion for life. My highest thanks.

A very special thank you goes to my book consultant, Ellen Reid, without whom this book simply would not have happened. Your gift at being able to discern who I am and what I wanted to bring forth with this manuscript are without equal. The people you then brought into my life to assist were each wonderful artisans: Laren Bright and his words, Dotti Albertine's design that gives the book its look and feel, and Bob Hankins whose passionate photography graces the book, web site and other aspects of the business. It took me a while to find you this time, Ellen. Next time, I'll begin with a conversation with you and save myself the aggravation!

Last and most importantly, I thank Lisa, my beloved bride. You trusted me from the beginning to find my own way through a difficult period and, without grasping, forcing, or ever rescuing me, loved me as I am and let this be enough! I began waking up when I saw you and my life has never been the same since. Your input, encouragement, and modeling of how to live life fully even when things occasionally fall apart inform me daily of how I want to be in this world. And, yes, I will follow through on the dinner at Arugula's.

# For Lisa

*You recognized*
*my Essence*
*when all I saw*
*were the wounds.*

DAN Holden has become an expert at transforming adversity into power in practical, tangible ways. Through personal experience with difficult transitions in his life, he deepened his spiritual connection and uncovered methods for showing others how to use the challenges in their lives to do the same, with greater elegance and ease. He writes, speaks and facilitates workshops from this solid foundation of someone who has walked through the fire.

Dan earned a bachelors degree in Psychology and a masters degree in Education. From eastern Kentucky and the urban ghettos of the Northeast to the management rooms of large corporations Dan's work has transformed people and teams. His message is that significant adversity shows up to change old ways of living and working that no longer serve us. If we're willing, it opens us to new, more elegant and powerful means.

From a successful career in counseling he moved to corporate life, and has since built a reputation of excellence in executive coaching, diversity work and facilitating workshops for leaders ranging from executives in Fortune 500 corporations to heads of independent companies. His specialty is walking into impossible situations and finding solutions in which people, teams and organizations prosper.

Dan Holden has co authored *Pathways to Partnership: The Leader's Journey from Patriarchy to Partnership*, a leadership development workshop, and *Mastering Leadership: The Inner Disciplines*, a twelve-week leadership curriculum on audio cassette. He is an ex-military paratrooper, an avid motorcyclist and outdoor enthusiast, a poet, an art lover, a husband, and father. He lives with his wife, Lisa, and their family in Connecticut, when he is not traveling, lecturing and leading workshops.

# Contents

THERE are times when the old way suddenly disappears. A job is lost, someone precious to you dies, or an accident causes you serious injury. A partner leaves. The friends you relied upon for support and encouragement move away. The enjoyable career you once thought defined you suddenly ends with a merger or downsizing, and you know in your gut that it will not return as it was. You earn a promotion but instead are fired. Or, you are promoted, and simultaneously lose all the recognition and camaraderie you wore only yesterday as a comforting blanket. You finally acknowledge that a loved one suffers from chemical addiction and you know their life *and your own* will never be the same. The body you took for granted becomes ill or has parts that will poorly function from here on out. You are lost.

You know something important has ended, and you must somehow go on, but the new way has not taken form. You see only darkness ahead and no path. The certainty and inward confidence with which you were moving so elegantly through life are lost. No matter where you look you cannot find them. They are burning out of you by a fire called *your life's mystery.* You don't know how or why this is happening. You are left only with doubt and fear. A numbness or despair creeps in where your drive and passion once lived. Nothing you do seems to make a difference and everything feels pointless and without meaning. Friends and colleagues have no words or comfort that reach you.

I have written this book for people who have lost important parts of their life and themselves, and, in the terrifying, lonely and disorienting space that follows, don't know what to do.

## ☽ *Interim Places*

If you are a spiritual person on this journey, as I am, the God within you when you entered this particular time and place will not be the God you have within you when you leave it. The spiritual concepts and understanding you once had will be forged in the fire of this place. Some may emerge stronger—like iron sharpened with higher iron—but others will be destroyed. Uncertainty lodges securely in your belly and throat. The feelings of aloneness and separation press in on every bone in your body and you wonder what you have done wrong to have ended up in such straights.

Some people enter these places but never come out. Sylvia Plath, Anne Sexton, and others come to mind. Others, like Christopher Reeves, seem to emerge stronger and more whole.

I call these *Interim Places,* the regions we wander through when the old ways are ending but before the new ways have taken form. They are the open, perilous landscapes in our lives, devoid of known reference markers that give our lives meaning, purpose, and a sense of belonging. Interim means "in between," but even this definition requires faith. We want to believe interim places are impermanent, like all other human experiences. But this notion is hard to maintain when everything we value is falling apart around us. An interim place feels as if it will last forever. It is wrapped in unbidden solitude and stillness that feel stronger than and beyond the reach of all the great forces of earth that move, shift, and change everything and everyone. This book will guide you and help make your way easier in interim places.

Interim places surprise us. We often do not know how they begin, or when, or why. We seldom believe we've chosen them. They come upon us when we are busy in our comfortable and obligated lives and open us in ways we never wanted to be opened before—yet so desperately needed to be. Severe disruptions bring unique gifts hidden in the center of them that cannot be found anywhere else. Like unwanted guests, they stand at the door of our guest house and ask to join us.

For many of us today, what we once looked to in the external world for a sense of self-worth and identity has disappeared or has been severely disrupted. Jobs, careers, homes, social standing, financial wealth, family stability, and the health of loved ones are some of the major reference points we examine to evaluate and answer the question, "How are we doing?" The sharp scythe of mergers, down sizings, reengineering, murder, disease, divorce, bankruptcy, and other forms of soul violence that permeate our culture have torn apart much of this infrastructure. This book describes how you can stand in your life when your external world falls apart. More importantly, you will learn how you can stand and emerge stronger and more whole, with genuine access to pragmatic, spiritual power. You will find these gifts are only in the center of interim places.

# ❭ The Sacred Self

I wish to affirm the possibility of a new kind of relationship with a higher, or sacred, self. During my own difficult passage, three spirit guides introduced themselves to me by name and spoke often of a new partnership, as your own guides may do with you if you ask for this. Because the guides are from another dimension of my experience, I don't see them or hear their voices. Rather, I sense their energy as one senses the presence of another person who enters a room but is out of view. Their initial entrance was quite real and alarming yet later became reassuring, like the company of good friends. This book argues that a new and real relationship with the sacred is possible for each of us and suggests practical ways to develop it. Stated more strongly: you can go no further into your life on your own strength. Spirit partnership is your new fuel.

Interim places are critical times for personal spiritual development, times where we can gain new found access to ourselves and to our spiritual dimension and power. The challenge I faced, and you may feel this way as well, is we seldom realize the gifts that are present for our taking when the disruptive and painful experience occurs. In fact, interim places feel like a waste of time, at best, and a terrifying open space of uncertainty, doom and unending separation from anything that matters. If transformation is possible, we are often dragged kicking and screaming into it! Yet, in the quiet spaces of breathing and resting, I found there is a community of spirit guidance—for myself and for each of us—whose voices and presence bring reassurance and hope to even the most desperate of conditions. My hope is that this story of contact with another dimension of self—the sacred dimension—will open for you a sustained, vital relationship with your own sacred self.

Upon entering the early landscape of Interim Place, you feel the staggering weight of your own aloneness in this life. You know no one can save you. None of the glossy books, Blockbuster videos, or lecture series on the "Three Quick and Easy Steps to Greatness, Wealth and Happiness" reached me when I stood in this place. The three spirit guides speak of the importance of losing attachments to the external world so our internal world can come into sharper focus. Each stage of our journey, however, seems like a descent into more treacherous, emotional terrain. The different terrains require an unusual range of learnable skills, grace and patience to negotiate, but they offer unmistakable gifts in return. The terrain of this internal landscape, the challenges and the gifts, along with tools and sacred self comments (in Chapters 2-6) will immediately reveal for you ways to move through a challenging time with renewed hope, skill and courage.

When my external world fell apart, I felt a strange combination of fear and disorientation. I wanted to die. You may experience similar emotions and not know what to do with them. Despite the love of a wonderful woman, I felt fundamentally unsure of myself and abandoned, a natural reaction to the loss of external props I had used to define my self and find value in my life. During this period, you experience three significant losses: Losing The Imaginary Self, The Figurine God, and A Sense of Place. I record my experience of these losses in Chapter 7. For those of us who learn to navigate through each loss, we may make a surprising discovery: we feel more alive than ever. Very alive. The guides said:

> The doorway to sacred partnership most always lies through experience we wish to reject. You enter through your vulnerability, not your power.

You slowly accept the fact that your real work is to live more in the present moment, grateful for your breath, life, and everything available for you to live. The poets and mystics speak of two lives. One is the life that each of us consciously lives each day and directs through choices we make and actions we take. The other is a deeper, essential life that remains largely unknown and mysterious, yet directs all manner of synchronicity and serendipity into our lives. Some call this the life of the soul, or the sacred self. Perhaps you are like me: I spent the first forty-five years of my life attempting with some success to carve out a life on my own terms. During interim places we experience life on our soul's terms. The great gift to discover is that which we fear will destroy us can bring us alive.

I have concerns about the language I've chosen to describe the sacred self. I see the sacred self as the aspect of us that is fully human yet simultaneously fully divine— spirit and light. It knows you fully because *it is you fully*, in this lifetime and all others. The sacred self also is one with God, the universe, the spirit, or any other name for the Great Other. I am eager to distinguish sacred from religious because my own experience is that this aspect of ours is not interested in definitional arguments. Of particular significance is my first experience of a Self separate from, yet in union with, my *personality*. Stated another way, in any situation there is much more happening than what your personality sees! There are other forces at play. In interim places, it is critical for you to learn how to recognize and move in harmony with these forces. The sacred self can be called upon to show you how to proceed.

Getting the personality off the throne seems central in transformation. Anyone who has hiked far into the American southwest, or has gotten lost in a rain forest or snowed in unexpectedly on a wilderness trek knows the same thing: you are simply visitors in a great land, amidst great forces and a community of beings that do not always or even usually recognize the claims of your personality attesting to your importance! The same dynamic applies to your interior life: there's much going on beyond your personality's ability to comprehend. You need other orientations, new ways of seeing and hearing, if you are to move forward in a healthier, more balanced way. This book is for you if this kind of learning is what you want.

In the midst of overwhelming uncertainty and fear, it is absurd for us to continue doing things as we have always done them. With practice, we slowly discover a quiet place within that remains at rest even when everything else around you is in turmoil. Each of us can find this place. This place of rest is our sacred self. Finding your way to this place is not always easy. The road maps presented here will help you find your own way to your sacred self and to the power, wisdom, and confidence that reside here.

Much of this book, and Chapter 8 in particular, centers around the discipline of opening the heart. The guides describe it this way:

*To open the heart is to open yourself to being fully human. This means opening to your essence, which is both human and spirit. Many people incorrectly assume that what distinguishes humans from other species is your intellect. While this perspective has an obvious element of truth here on earth in this time dimension, your intellect is not what distinguishes you elsewhere in the universe or on earth in other time dimensions. Countless other beings and civilizations have greater intellectual capacities than humans. Nevertheless, the entire created universe knows of you because of your heart—where you make choices and express gratitude for your life experience on earth. It is also the place within you where God abides and speaks with you and where you recognize and respond to truth and beauty.*

*Everyone has a sacred center, a higher self. Everyone has guides assigned them for the journey. Even if your experience to date tells you otherwise, we say "Choose to know these aspects of who you are." Then, relinquish this choice to the universe with no strings attached as to how the response must take place. Remain vigilant. Expect a response. Time, energy flow, and your ability to sense the movement of spiritual forces in and around you are all changing very quickly. Set aside your past experience, and be open to today. Experiment, and trust your own process. This time in your life is for discovery. Take a first step or a next step. You will be met.*

The sacred self is still a powerful stranger to many of us. It's not found by looking out in the external world but into the inner world, which slowly becomes visible as external attractions slip away. The sacred self and the guides are responsible for writing about our new partnership with one another in Chapter 1, how we achieved it and how you can too. The bottom line for you and me is this: a relationship with our sacred self truly allows us to see ourselves more clearly, and step more humbly into each day to live the life and make the contribution we came here for.

Interim places carve deep grooves in you and leave you with a different way of relating to your life and power. I discovered I had been secretly hoping for some marvelous lightning bolt of insight about how to quickly acquire wealth and success and all manner of material and physical abundance. It hasn't happened yet, but something more powerful and sustaining has. One more time, I saw how all my drives and definitions are steeped in the American popular culture. This time, I smiled and wrote about what I know: *We experience inner shifts in consciousness before we make external shifts in what we do.* Standing on the shore of this new terrain, I felt a freedom I had never known. Chapters 9 through 11 provide a glimpse of this new land and how you can move into it.

I know that my experience in interim places is not mine alone. Many others face similar challenges each day. My hope is that this experience will cause you to slow down and reflect on the time you are in and, perhaps, help you find rest in the midst of the turmoil. There are two crises happening now: the one outside of you that defies your attempts to control it and the one inside you, where you actually live and breathe. You may have seldom looked inwardly before now and, unfortunately, missed out on the gifts given there. It was not time then. Now is your time to look.

—*Dan Holden*

# Waking Up

*One day the silence you feared*
*runs up to you like a thief*
*you have eluded all these years.*
*He takes everything.*
*Standing there without the coat*
*of success and friends and activity*
*you are lost.*
*Forget about instant deliverance.*
*If God were here that's what He would say*
*but He is only the stone ground*
*you fall upon*
*and you fear that's all*
*He ever was.*
*Clothed for the first time*
*only in silence*
*you discover how strange you are*
*to yourself*
*like the newborn you brought home*
*and searched all night.*
*Angel's hair, closed eyes, tiny fingers and toes,*
*the soft, smooth skin folded around the elbows,*
*the secret kissing spot on the back of the neck,*
*frighteningly rapid breath and a sweet smell*
*unlike anything you had ever known.*
*You knew then you would love her*
*forever and tonight, alive in your own*
*staggering silence*
*you have never looked more beautiful,*
*or completely magnificent*
*as you really are.*

—D.H.

### CHAPTER 1

# Partnership with the Sacred Self

Standing still and hearing the voice of spirit

LIVING fully requires that we learn to die well, and many times. Things end and we must loosen our grasp and allow them to pass. Circumstances we cannot control show up in our lives as unbidden houseguests demanding a visit of uncertain duration. We may persist in holding on to the past and forcing a future we think we want until we are weighed down with exhaustion, bitterness and grief. Only then do we let go in desperation. Dying well does not come easily. Yet it is exactly what our world, our co-workers, our partners, lovers and family require of us if we are to live with a full and opened heart. Only then will we see that allowing and releasing are not doorways to death but secret openings to new and very different possibilities. This is what the angels, the spirit guides, have given me to say to you.

I resisted their guidance for as long as I could.

I built a good and successful life. I work as a consultant to people and organizations, serving as a teacher and healer. My clients include managers of large, famous corporations as well as "normal" people who go to work each day in organizations of all sizes. The central experience I write about in these pages is not unique to me even though I felt very isolated and abnormal as I experienced it. The dream came crashing down. I was left behind, very lost and afraid. What do we do when important things end? How can we stand and grow stronger in the midst of events that bring us such fear and uncertainty? Do we rebuild the original dream or create something new?

If our lives are a journey, then this is a story about a place in the journey where everything that once worked for you no longer works! The knowledge you've acquired and come to trust fails you. The competencies, strengths and personal qualities you've built a life and career around fall short. This time feels as though a massive, destructive force had slammed into you. I came to realize, as you may, it can also become a time of extraordinary healing and restoration.

This terrifying place marks the beginning of your deeper life. It is the territory in which leaders who leave a positive and lasting mark on us in our families, communities and work places are developed. Since this experience is one that you quite naturally wish to avoid, my hope is to offer guideposts along the way so you can navigate this terrain a little easier than I did, more faithfully, and find the secret gifts more quickly than was true for me. That there are gifts hidden in hardship is not a new concept; that you have a community of beings around you whose work is to skillfully guide you into the life you've come here to live, and equip you with new competencies and power with which to live, may be a very new concept for you. It was for me.

My choice to write about a difficult passage that I normally would have kept hidden was a direct result of two very surprising events. The first occurred one morning as I was in my office. The year before I entered interim places I began a daily discipline of writing "morning pages." I fill three blank notebook pages with whatever is in me to write about. Most of it is noise, most of it useless, and some of it very insightful and extremely relevant. The first chapter and title of this book first appeared in my "morning pages." All of it, over the years, has been an important way for me to remain grounded in the real stuff of my life each day.

## ❯ *Hearing the voice of Spirit*

After five months of writing I was startled one morning by the sudden appearance of three distinctly different energy fields. It felt like walking into your home where you know someone else is there, too (children, partner, etc.) but you don't know who. The energy is different when another presence is near. The energy shift was very real even for me, for someone who doesn't attend to energy fields. I stopped writing, asked who was present, and wrote down what came to me at that moment. It happened just this casually!

These energy fields (that's how they felt to me—real yet formless personalities) identified themselves as three master guides who were here to assist me through this period in my life. They each had different areas of expertise yet were one with each other and worked in union both with Spirit and with me. Elihu spoke of deep integration of who I am in this lifetime; this work seems to have to do with bringing all of me into deeper union with myself and with my sacred self. Zenig's work is focused on issues of destiny and purpose; these issues have much to do with remembering and recognizing who I really am and what I came here to do. Telios works with me around partnership with the sacred, higher self. I suspect much of the work I struggle with around ego attachments to external things was quietly guided through Telios. I first heard about partnership with the sacred self through the guides.

Their advice to me was straightforward: "Stand still, you are safe."

The second surprising event was my life began to crumble in ways it never had. And so did I. More about this later.

Your own encounter with guidance is very easy to make happen. First, decide if this is something you want. If you had this relationship, what would it give you that is important to you? What would it feel like for you to have these results? Then, you simply state your intention verbally, i.e., "I would like to open a connection with my spirit guidance . . . and I would like you to confirm your presence in ways I can understand and recognize." Then go about your life while quietly paying attention to what happens. Soon, you will have your confirmation!

I have not spoken like this about my guides before. I do not come out of a New Age spirituality and I have little patience for the esoteric tricks and short cuts I stereotypically associate with this brand of personal development. The guides, as I refer to them, have been private teachers or coaches up to this point and I want to be clear about how I see their relationship. It does not matter to me if you believe in guides or not. While I assume everyone has guidance of some sort in and around them, I cannot prove this nor do I want to bother. Guidance is an invaluable part of your road ahead, so take what seems valid to you and don't get too hung up on the rest.

- ➤ Guides are both a part of you and also not your personality.

- ➤ They seldom distinguish or call attention to themselves or to their work except in response to direct questions from you. Even then, they may not answer. They appear to be utterly uninterested in themselves but deeply interested in you.

➤ They are one with God / Spirit / Life Force / The Universe / Higher Power however you understand these terms, and yet are themselves too.

➤ They abide with your sacred self in and around you in an unseen dimension of yourself. You don't have to go into another dimension to find them but instead, by being quiet and by paying attention to what is always present, they can be discerned.

➤ You may experience no emotion when you converse with them and frequently will dismiss what they say as something you yourself could say. To this they once responded: "We make your own true wisdom available to you; if it sounds familiar we say, 'Good'."

➤ They honor your spiritual traditions and challenge you to expand the small boxes you put God in. {I write from a Judeo-Christian perspective.}

➤ They honor choices you make yet continually work towards what is highest for you and for all others who are impacted by your choices. They are not simple gift givers and miracle workers but work in the deeper waters of your life to draw forth all of who you are and what is yours.

➤ When you seek wisdom or further direction you may have the experience of going within for the answer, not outside of yourself. This feels important to say because much of my own Judeo-Christian education and practice supported an external, hierarchical view of God. I looked up and outside of myself for answers. This notion does not fit as well anymore and, in fact, may have created some of the unhealthy dependency and attachments I have written about. The old view may not help you move towards a closer partnership with the sacred. In it you remain separate, below and less than what you truly are.

## ❯ Stillness and aloneness: strange doorways to community with the Sacred Self

It seems ironic to me that during a time when you can feel so alone, the underlying agenda in interim places is to befriend and come to know the sacred self. Your essence.

Early in this period of my life I made a startling discovery. I noticed that while I was frightened by the financial and emotional crisis I was in, there was an aspect of me which remained quite calm through it all. This aspect seemed content to observe and note how I was feeling and little else. I referred to this place within as the "Sleeping Jesus" part of me, after the biblical story of a storm at sea that threatened to capsize the boat in which Jesus and his disciples rode. These fishermen disciples, who made their living on the water, were terrified by the fierceness of the storm. It must have been an extraordinary storm! Jesus slept in the back of the boat until his boat mates woke him up and cried to him to do something. He got up and told the storm to be quiet. It did.

I wish all deliverance came this quickly and gallantly. This calm witness within is your sacred self. You can find your way here when you step back from the noise of your life and recognize there is someplace and someone within not noisy or distracted at all.

Your sacred self is best accessed in stillness and quietness but is very active and involved with you all the time.You may at any time race ahead with your own plans and designs or you can enter in dialogue with this source within and work in partnership. When I choose the latter, I am frequently surprised by the results. The universe uses all the resources available to answer our questions and respond to our needs and concerns, not just through spoken language, although as I explain below, spoken dialogue with the sacred self is possible too.

Your relationship with your sacred self brings great benefits. For example, at this point I routinely have clear guidance on work projects that has resulted in consistently favorable outcomes. I have had entire conference designs dumped into my lap, where I simply needed to record what I had seen. Other times, on a walk or run, I will find sudden resolution of a pressing dilemma. Impossible obstructions suddenly have a way through them, but only as I quiet myself and listen within. I have heard ways to say sensitive things when in dialogue with others that I know did not originate in my head. I have received help, encouragement and direction from trees, rivers, birds, and various animals who have showed up as signs or messages that were timely for me. In fact, as we learn to open our heart and become more conscious of this presence within, there is guidance virtually everywhere.

This core place within you is a place of impossible love, an open fire burning in deep water, a place in which you know you are held in love and truth. From this place all good things flow and all good things you want to create originate here. When God (in whatever way you understand God) speaks to you, the guidance is received in this place, for it is the only place large and spacious enough to receive the light of love and wisdom that belongs to you. This quiet presence is your higher or sacred self. Your guides are here to show you the way home!

This book is an account of the exchange between me and

my sacred self during a terrifying time of disruption and change. As a teacher and healer, I know now that my work is to show the way to invoke, call forth and unfold this vital connection with our own divinity.

Poets and mystics have said for centuries there are forces within us we know nothing about; that they are there for our good, not our destruction. The German poet, Rainier Rilke, compares this force to a fierce and relentless enemy which lays siege to our life. It is able to move quietly like the tide through our defenses and break down walls of separation that keep us from our own life and destiny. The great Sufi mystic Rumi speaks of this core life within us as an artist within who's not interested in how things look differently in the moonlight. Clearly, our deeper life has an agenda of its own.

Your calling and mine is to belong to this inner world in ways most of us have yet to do. We are very enmeshed and content in our successful lives when the bottom falls out. Interim places are the doorways into a deeper life of purpose and belonging but they don't resemble doorways we are familiar with. Interim places begin where our power ends, so we enter through our vulnerability and woundedness, not our strength. We seldom enter consciously. We've grown accustomed to a small number of familiar friends at our guest house; interim places invite us to expand the guest list!

As I continue to learn, the capacity to form a vital, real partnership of different equals is a critical outcome of my extended stay in interim places. My guides and my sacred self will work with me as I attempt to describe what this partnership is all about.

## ❱ The Sacred Self observes

*Humans come into this life with a built in desire to know the sacred, the source of their own being. They desire to know and belong again to the home of their origin, to have clarity about their own purpose and mission, and to know their life and time here have meaning. They would prefer pleasure over pain, and quickly attach themselves to that which affords pleasure and avoid those things that bring pain and suffering. Much of what is learned in the early years of life in your culture centers on becoming more independent and self directive so as to enable you to survive alone in the world.*

*Meaning is seen as residing in things that must be accomplished or acquired in the world. Status, prestige, value are assigned to these things. Importantly, people learn to assign worth and value to themselves based on how big, how much, how often, how long, how high, how active, how busy, how fast they can move in their world. God, in this paradigm, is seen as a presence who assists people in navigating through this world successfully. God becomes attached to success and advancement even as humans themselves do. Failure, struggle, loss are seen as tragic and appeals are made to God who, it is hoped, will intervene and set people back in the safety and comfort for which they long. Good times bring praise, but tough times seldom illicit the same sense of gratitude.*

*We say these things without judgment. There are many variations to the story above but in your culture this seems to be a predominant pattern.*

*What we want to say to you is that we love you and honor who you are. To us, it seems that people fail to genuinely record, in their bones and bellies, just how beautiful, magnificent, and honored they are and how they are seen in this light by the sacred. By God. Stated another way, you are each prized and cherished as you are and are held to be of far greater value than you can imagine. There are no other beings anywhere in the universe more honored than you.*

*When those of you who see yourselves on a spiritual path or quest ask for assistance, we see this as a time to open you to who you truly are—your magnificence. Your complexity. The sacred essence that is in the center of you. We work to open your capacity to experience the fullness of who you are, your vision and your despair, your courage and your cowardice, your love and your fear. To this end we speak here of the work of self compassion and self love. It is the work of developing yourself as a sacred partner. It is work of the highest value to us in this dimension because it requires that you come to know and handle yourself with the same reverence with which you are created.*

*There is a new partnership available to people today because there is a new energy for partnership available on earth. There is considerable hunger for it. The emphasis on involvement, team work, community building, consensus, collaboration, dialogue all speak to the growing awareness that you are all connected to one another in ways never before imagined. This sense of connection to and need to work in alignment with others as partners extends to the spirit realm as well. You each have a sacred self and spirit guides to assist you. You may ask for verification of these words and receive it!*

*In the old paradigm, humans frequently gave assent to a concept called, "God's Will" and professed a desire to know and pursue it. In the day-to-day matters of life however, humans often pursue their own agenda independently. Again, the covert aspect of this agenda was largely about the pursuit of pleasure and the avoidance of pain. Much good often came out of this independent action. But something was missing.*

*In the quiet place of the heart there remains the original desire for union with the sacred and for walking and working in alignment, as partners. Many would be surprised to know there is no plan that God made for them; there are instead plans that you and God jointly created and agreed to prior to your lifetime. These plans are for your good, not for your destruction. These plans are about your living to the fullness of who you are and coming into true abundance in all areas of your life, beginning with your relationship with your self.*

*Our agenda, in the sacred dimension (as you call it) is to assist you with this work. To help you find and abide in the sacred center of your self where the Spirit / Life Force / Christ Spirit dwells in union with you. From this place all things are indeed possible. In this place within, you have all that you need to generate all that you desire, all that you are, all that your purpose and mission here require of you. Yes, there is much to learn about this sacred place of union within, but even knowing this is already present and complete. Apart from this place of union with the sacred, you can do nothing. In fact, you can no longer do what you once could do alone. The time for independent action has passed.*

*We ask those of you who desire partnership with the sacred presence within to make your intention known. Speak your intention and choose to open yourself to the partnership loudly, perhaps in the presence of supportive others. Then, in your own style find ways to do the following things on a regular basis:*

➤ QUIET YOURSELF AND FIND TIMES FOR STILLNESS. Walk, sit, drive, write to yourself, listen. It does not matter what form your quiet takes; your intention to find quiet will attract the best ways to you. Be patient with yourself. It may take a few weeks or several months to get started. The deeper changes that begin to happen in you are subtle, virtually invisible and hard to track. They defy most attempts to evaluate, which often means you will feel as if nothing is happening. Actually, much is happening. Choices and directions for action made in this space are often aligned with your own sacred self and have great potency.

➤ EXPERIENCE AND FEEL EVERYTHING, WITHOUT JUDGMENT. Your culture prescribes what is valid for you to feel. The prescription is too small and leaves many people feeling unnecessarily inadequate and inferior. Feelings are simply energy passing through your body. Learn to allow yourself the honor of being fully human, an individual capable of experiencing the full range of feeling without shrinking back or lapsing into self blame and judgment. Negative feelings often conceal unhealthy attachments, early wounds, and so forth. Experience it all and allow it to pass through and out of you. This stance is especially important with regard to quieting yourself. Notice the noise and allow it to go its way. Remember, experiences and feelings that feel worthless and foolish are often the gateway to the sacred.

➤ ACKNOWLEDGE EVERYTHING WITHOUT JUDGMENT. Our intention here is remind you of the power of your spoken word used here to simply describe your experience. "I feel angry . . . I want to slam the door in his face . . . I feel shamed . . ." This discipline allows you to acknowledge that an experience is part of you while at the same time naming it distinguishes it from you. In the sacred realm, the one who names is more powerful than that which is named. It is a powerful spiritual practice to stand in the midst of an upsetting experience and name what is going on within you. It makes you stronger and affords distance and light between you and your experience. The path to opening the heart is to allow all experience and all feeling to be valid. It is also the way into your compassion since you will find it harder to judge others when you have acted or felt like they have.

➤ CHOOSE WHAT YOU WANT IN YOUR LIFE AND THEN SURRENDER THESE MATTERS TO THE SACRED BUT REMAIN VIGILANT AND ATTENTIVE. Surrendering does not mean giving up on a matter. Rather, you are inviting in help and resources from another dimension and looking for their input, help and support. It is how partners work with one another. Remember that we use resources that are already available as well as all manner of other resources. Know that you have been heard. Continue to allow attachments to preferred solutions or to "how things must be" to slip away.

➤ MOVE FORWARD AND DO WHAT YOU KNOW TO DO TODAY. Once you have done the above there is really nothing else for you to do. Just allow yourself to be in an expectant, interested, and hopeful stance but do not limit yourself or us to one way of responding to or solving the dilemma. We work with "time" and resources in ways that are different than you do. Anything can happen and it is possible for solutions to be there that you neither see nor imagine right now, because it is not time for them to show up for you. Yet they exist in another realm as completed solutions because nothing here exists in an incomplete, fragmented state.

We wish to speak further about the phrase, 'Do what is in you to do today.' This phrase is drawn from the author's experience during a half marathon road race when we challenged his excessive self demands for high performance with the advice to 'Run the race that is within you to run today.' Immediately, the weight of expectation lifted and he was free to enjoy the rest of the run. In your culture it is important to note that he ran well too, and finished better than he expected. From our perspective, it is essential to "be" in right relationship with your sacred self so that you are able to allow the "doing of today" to show itself, and then receive it and move with it.

Your culture is a doing culture. Partnership with both Spirit and the sacred self includes an emphasis on being. Only then does the doing flow out from the relationship and the deep knowing between partners. Too much of the frenetic activity of your culture is independently generated and appears driven by an unconscious need to fill the vacuum created by a non- vital relationship with the sacred self. Many are out of alignment with who they really are. What terrible thing would befall the soul who chose to do less!

Some days, there are really only one or two things that need doing. A connection needs to be made between you and another, for example. A phone call. A short minute of encouragement to someone. A moment to gaze out the window, breathe deeply, and express gratitude for your health and well being. A moment to genuinely acknowledge and then surrender a stressful dilemma. A brief talk in which you engage the heart of another person in a way that leaves both of you refreshed. A moment to feel the energy of what you feel, then smile, and allow it to pass through you. In our economy here, any one of these could be your true work today and you would accomplish much were these done. To ride the deeper waters of sacred partnership requires a raft that floats, not a power boat. Learn to inquire early each day as to what needs to be done that day. Listen to your deeper knowing.

We speak of a simpler way to be in your life. In this way, attachments that link your worth and value to how much you do are allowed to pass away. This simpler way, however, is not easy. Your relationship with the sacred self (where we reside and speak with you) is destined to become one of unencumbered joy, yet this joy rests on the other side of attachments that ensnare you. Know only this: we are with you and assist you every step of the way. The human boy or girl, man or woman, is of unsurpassed beauty, radiance and honor. It is universally impossible for a human to go through this earth journey alone, separated from love and loving help. Reflect on these words often: it is universally impossible to go through your journey alone. You have much help. Ask to experience it.

We have given practical guidelines here to help you navigate into these relationship waters. We wish to say to you that the partnership available to each of you is far greater and holds more hope and promise than we have conveyed with these guidelines. To experience yourself as a divine being, a co-partner with the sacred, a center of a marvelous community of beings here to honor you and work with you is a great thing. To know even in your loneliest moments that you are not alone, that support is there and that even the most troubling dilemmas can be rectified is what people experience in their partnerships with the spirit within.

Beyond problem solving, however, is the development of a loving trust between us, a certain nimbleness of movement you begin to see in yourself that allows you to move and stand still as needed, take action and allow conditions to change on their own at just the right times so that no action is wasted. You begin to feel whole and nourished all of the time; rested, confident and capable of being the spiritual warrior and light being you came here to be. These developments far exceed the steps we mention above and bring an abiding joy, excitement and confidence to you that others will see and be drawn to.

I offer these words as comfort to you who are moving through very difficult experiences now. You know only loss and fear and there are no promises or guarantees for the path ahead. In the most trying of circumstances, the path itself disappears, as it did with me, and we are left to stumble alone seeking anything to hang onto for balance. We find nothing . . . or so it seems.

# ☽ *Tools for the Journey*

### How to establish relationship with your sacred self

➤ State your intention out loud, "I want to open a relationship with my sacred self, my essence."

➤ Open to the concerns and fears you might experience and share these with your sacred self and with another person. If you come from a religious background you might experience the sacred self as idolatry. Share this and ask for direction. I see the sacred self as my essence, the core place within me that God most easily speaks to and hears me back. My mind and personality are too easily distracted with other things.

➤ Ask for proof of this connection and then pay attention. Your proof will likely come very quickly and in ways unique to you.

➤ Find a way of getting quiet for a few minutes on a regular basis and making contact. Speaking, writing, walking, sitting in nature are good places to start.

➤ Say 'yes' quickly to small indicators that your life is out of balance and that attention is needed in your heart. Increases in stress, irritation, anger, small accidents and injuries, coupled with feelings of having to push too hard to make even small things turn in a desired direction are sometimes secret openings to the sacred, indicators that you better stop and reflect.

➤ Pay special attention to feelings of loneliness, sadness, and a longing that is hard to describe to others. Sometimes, as our spirit (sacred self) draws close, we experience this as a hunger for connection.

# Saving Yourself

*One day all the color drains from*
*the brilliant gold and green cornfields.*
*The azure blue and deep purple*
*wildflowers disappear.*
*The old oak trees in the neighborhood turn gray,*
*and the dark green and silver water*
*in the reservoir bleeds dry.*
*The geese turn to fly south*
*and do not return.*

*The old way has ended.*

*You see only uncertainty ahead*
*and know it will shatter*
*your hidden sanctuary*
*with its cold blade of fear.*

*It does.*

*The piercing, though, feels familiar,*
*like a remembered smell*
*from the fields when you were a boy.*
*You have been lost and lonely for a long time.*
*In one instant you know what your body*
*has tried to tell you in all of those days*
*when you were away.*
*It cannot lie.*

*In the silence now arriving*
*You weep with a sweet joy—*
*the joy of knowing how easy it is*
*to miss your own life*
*while living another.*

*—D.H* [1]

### CHAPTER 2

## The Emotional Landscape of Interim Places
Discovering the central task in trauma: saving yourself

SEVERAL developments marked the entrance to my interim place: the end of a twenty-year marriage; an unexpected downturn in my consulting practice, resulting in a serious financial downturn; the departure of good friends who moved away; and an extended time of solitude away from friends, family, or clients. These events spanned roughly eighteen months. Individually, none of these factors seems unusually harsh or significant. Many other people have experienced the same or worse. In hostile parts of the world, every day is more of a struggle than my quiet life here in the United States. Yet, we have our own brand of desperation here behind the concrete and glass, the lush lawns and shopping malls. Sometimes ordinary events trigger deep change in us because *we experience them differently. We're ready to be touched and impacted in a different way.* This was the case for me. I experienced everything as an assault on my identity as a man, as a father, as a person of worth and value.

I have always been clear about what I wanted in life and how to get it. I had a very strong sense, however, that something profound would happen in my work approximately one year before the bottom fell out of my consulting practice. I felt called to teach and heal people of their fear and doubt about walking the life of faith. I wanted to teach about an inner sacred presence that was the source of all power and supply, all resourcing and sufficiency. I felt this guiding presence and wanted others to feel it as well. This dynamic internal presence was what I always wanted the church to explore and help people to experience directly and consistently. I felt disappointed when it offered dogma and doctrine as substitutes for having an experiential relationship with God. I was very clear about all of this until my own inner confidence vanished.

My father's alcoholism was a scalpel that cut a lonely wedge in my boyhood life. I resented him, and I resented the God I heard about in church whom they packaged so nicely in clean, understandable linen, which frankly tore apart under the weight of my young but real world.

What I wanted then was what most of us wanted as children and want now as adults: life on our own terms. Clothed with this kind of power, I reasoned my basket would brim over with abundance, and I would never experience scarcity. I would only have good times drenched with prosperity and satisfaction. Comfort and pleasure. Does God have bad days? If God doesn't, why should I? I felt that this permanent oasis of good days was a legitimate request and that people who stood in my way should be eliminated. Or at least avoided. Early on I came to love the feelings of happiness and to despise and feel ashamed of any negative feelings. I was convinced God must have looked at me in similar ways.

As absurd as this sounds, most families and organizations offer plenty of support for feeling this way . I attempted to ride the rapids of my life with this positive fuel. Like so many others do, I made it about forty years down river before I realized something was faulty. This positive fuel was never designed to take me that far, but rather to help me survive my early family years. I thought I had learned this, but I realize now, I hadn't learned it deeply enough. As children of families skilled in distortion and deception, most of what we learn about ourselves and the world must be unlearned later. Interim places are where these early strategies are dealt a death blow.

## ❯ *Secret openings, hidden doorways*

When you are in traumatic transition everything can become blurry and disorienting. This is because the old way is ending and you need new reference markers to find your way. You cannot persist in forcing your old way without causing damage to yourself and others. Secret openings, hidden doorways are early (emotional and behavioral) warning signposts that indicate that you are closing in on an ending of some sort and that your spirit wants your attention:

➤ Your emotions begin to run wild. Anger, frustration, fear begin to crowd your thoughts.

➤ Depression begins to find a lodging place in your gut; you lose energy and focus and have a harder time simply showing up in your life each day. This can express itself either in heightened levels of anxiety, anger, melancholy, or lethargy.

➤ No matter how long you sleep you still feel exhausted and there doesn't seem to be any objective reason why. You may have felt this way when there were unusually demanding times at work or at home in the past; this time though, it feels differently for you.

➤ You begin to wonder what all of this means and no answer satisfies you. This may or may not be the first time you've asked yourself these questions; it doesn't matter. This time the questions feel relentless to you. No amount of extra work, exercise, drinking, sex, busyness or community involvement makes the questions go away. They demand your attention!

➤ Circumstances at work or at home begin to shift in ways that feel uncomfortable. Efforts at addressing them don't seem to work. More importantly, you experience a secret wish that things continue to play out as they are. Stated another way, at deeper levels you feel a "rightness" about all of this.

These are some of the salient signposts the spirit often gives us when significant change is on the horizon. Think of them as early warning signs given to you so you can prepare for change. What is called for here is not fear but inviting the spirit to be a part of it all. From the start, your sacred self wants to walk with you through this new terrain and help you make new road maps for yourself.

**The road maps we carry are outdated.**

In childhood and adolescence, we each draw unconscious mental maps we think will serve us well for the path ahead. Twenty-five years later, I was still approaching my marriage and management circles with my childhood maps in hand. You may have the same experience. The organizations which employ us are all too willing to support us in our delusions because they run on many of the same assumptions. We still use these early strategies even though we built them long ago to help us gain a sense of control during a time in our lives when we had none.

The boundaries of your outdated map may look something like mine:

➤ Act happy.

➤ Act like you have your act together.

➤ Keep very secret the dark and fearful, sensual and passionate parts.

➤ Disregard any negative experiences, or, if you must, fix them quickly and move on. If you can't, you are weak.

➤ Fall in line.

➤ If you feel discomfort, fear or caution keep it to yourself.

➤ Connect your worth directly to your performance, and always perform well.

➤ Remember that what your friends think of you is more important than what you think of yourself, so continue to perform well.

➤ If you have trouble with any of these boundaries, keep it to yourself; it means something is wrong with you. Closely guard this secret, though; after all, no one else seems to be struggling.

➤ Always hold onto control; if you lose it you will lose everything valuable and never get it back.

➤ Assume that any uncomfortable emotion means something is bad about you; ignore it, deny it, keep moving and don't look at it.

➤ Compensate for any secret feeling of inferiority by over-achieving, over-controlling or over-pleasing important people in your life; this way your secret inferiority will remain secret.

**Your body is not your enemy. The wisdom you want is hidden within. Make friends quickly!**

Being human means being vulnerable. It means you are temporarily housed in a body that others can hurt. The body has a capacity and a need for feeling everything, coupled with a memory that *forgets nothing*. I let God know that the whole idea of housing humans in bodies was a big mistake. Big mistake. My early church years confirmed what I already knew: If it were not for the body and its feelings, being God-like for us humans would be much easier. Being a boss, a spouse, or a mother or father would also be easier, I believed, if we didn't have to contend with the body of our humanity. Just think of how much longer you could work if you didn't have a body that got tired! Imagine how much easier it would be to hide your true feelings if you didn't have feelings that knot your stomach and tighten your shoulders or if your body didn't *remember everything*.

If you're like me, you are woefully wrong about all this! With luck, you can catch yourself before you are lost completely. The universe is demanding but compassionate enough to send you through interim places to learn about your true beauty and the power contained in your body. It's in times of apparent weakness that you will open to and more easily see your divine beauty and power, located in the center of you. That's what these signposts, your guidance and sacred self are here to assist you with.

**The secret openings and hidden doorways we will talk about throughout this passage are often given to us, registered in our body.**

I thought I knew about these things, but, as I look back, it's clear I knew nothing.

# ❯ *Tools for the Journey*

### How to recognize interim places

Your emotional state, described earlier, has begun to grow more troublesome. There are real and imagined external changes that have triggered your feelings. Some of the external shift may be sudden, as in an accident or a loss of a job. Other times conditions change gradually without you knowing it, as when friends and colleagues leave one by one for other opportunities. Your base of support and recognition has dried up without anyone raising a flag. Your life as an adult is primarily a life of transitions. New schools, new work places, new relationships, new bosses, new homes, all challenge you to remain open and attentive. There is no immunity to change. You can believe all of this yet struggle deeply with the harsh realities of interim places. There is a unique mix of wild, life threatening elements that make this time more upsetting than all other times of change you have faced.

As I work with others in similar periods of deep change, several patterns emerge that mark the entrance into interim places:

➤ Basic life systems are threatened. Your health, home, family, core relationships, finances appear to be directly at risk.

➤ Current or anticipated sources of your supply dry up or disappear altogether. Financial resources are lost; medical strategies and resources fail; a partner leaves and does not come back.

➤ Your proven strategies for recovery no longer work for you. Industriousness, effort, hard work and will power no longer seem to matter at all but instead yield greater degrees of frustration.

➤ Your capacity to remain present to the demands and joys of each day slowly but unmistakingly erodes, giving way to the suffocating sand storms of an imagined and terrifying future. The loss of this capacity to simply be present is especially felt at night, or in other quiet moments. Mental noise makes sleep difficult. Frustration slowly gives way to fear and then despair.

➤ Momentary gains are washed out with further losses and longer periods of unbidden solitude and uncertainty. Quick attempts to fix the situation, to right the sinking ship of your life, fail to yield lasting results. Things grow better then turn sharply worse.

➤ At some point fear becomes the predominant emotion you feel each day as you grip your life tighter and tighter thinking your grasp will make you safe.

Name the changes you experience now and the feelings generated in you. Slow down, invite spirit into this time. Do this now even though your mind tells you it is a waste of time.

I hesitate to write this description because it sounds so bleak: Make no mistake, interim places are very difficult times because of the demands they make on you to stop the activity and busyness of your life and attend to matters in a very different way. Many organizations could benefit from the same call to "STOP" the way they conduct meetings, make decisions, hire and develop people, and manage bad news. To do so, however, requires a willingness to turn and

face what can only feel like a bleak, uncertain, task. It is
sometimes easier to avoid it altogether.

## ❯ *Fear or love: where will you spend your days?*

When you have worked enough in corporate settings, you
know that you work from a place of either fear or love. All
action that originates from fear invariably results over time
in maintaining the status quo. Designed to move you away
from discomfort, fear-based action often brings about the
very consequences it seeks to avoid. This is especially true
in interim places.

Ultimately, when events begin to dismantle your life,
you return to the central strategy of exhausting work sched-
ules, impossible priorities, no rest, and—now more than
ever before—little or no resources. You work faster but often
only on the surface of issues. You may meet continually
with others but seldom engage them in substantive dialogue. Substitutes for the real thing. The alternative—living
and working from a stance of deep commitment and
desire—can lead to very different results that are much closer to who you are and to what you actually want. But very
few people, myself included, wade into these waters.

Fear stops us. Fear has often stopped me. Interim places
invite you to come to terms with both your fear and love,
and decide which master you wish to serve. It is important
to choose how you want to be during this time and how you
want to be at the end. Love or fear are the options.

If illness or injury has brought you to the edge of great
change, you may study your conditions with great vigor
while all the time attempting to keep your life running as it
has always run. You return to old habits and their magnetic
pull on your life. Interim places take away your ability to

return. There is only one option: go forward into your unknown. Even though this means facing your fear, you do so out of love for life, for wholeness, to finally be at home with yourself and opened to community with others.

Early on, if you are sincere, you recognize the turbulent waters ahead. You know that to turn away from them and busy yourself elsewhere would be a serious mistake. Turning inward to face yourself and your life, however, feels like death to you. The soul has its own agenda, and your momentary comfort is usually not high on its priority list. It wants you to fully embody the life you came here to live. We each come here with a purpose, a contribution to make that only we can make. Sometimes this purpose is something we do, grand and public, or small and unwitnessed. Sometimes it is apart from anything we do; it is how we are, within our being and state of consciousness. We do not rest until we somehow stumble upon this purpose and commit ourselves to it.

**Lofty thoughts. None of this matters to you now.**

My love for control, wrapped in an entrepreneurial capacity for self-employment, had brought me to this moment in my life. Looking back, the one right choice I made—and that you must make—was to fully experience myself and this time. I no longer wanted to remain hidden from myself and others. I felt the gravity pull of my heart and chose to honor it. I knew this time it was intimately linked with my purpose in life, but it would be many, many months before I could begin to glimpse what the link was.

Your purpose is rarely the path you see clearly and choose freely. During this time, you know and feel little more than fear and a sense of being utterly lost in your own life. Interim places are inner places that fill you with great uncertainty and disruption. They ambush you. You suddenly find yourself in strange and terrifying emotional land-scapes that are as real as any external threat you've encountered. It is as if wrestling with this inner landscape brings out of hiding the real issues of your soul. How you move in this landscape determines how you move anywhere. What you greet head-on tends to dissolve as an item on your life's horizon; what you deny or avoid tends to come back repeatedly, seeking your acknowledgement.

This time can feel like a slow-moving earthquake beneath your feet, disrupting the life-affirming waterways and emotional landscape of your life. It exposes your humanity, the rawest essence that would-be gods and wounded warriors like us do not want to observe. Little of what you read is useful. The self-help books are too tame, too rational, too confident, and fixed in their recipes to even come close to explaining what you feel now. This place is a canyon carved by a mysterious, deep current in your life that requires you to fully experience life's events and clearly learn the gift of your humanity. Or die.

I indeed felt like I was dying. I hated the early days of this period quickly, completely, and continually. And you may too.

## ❯ *The four terrains of interim places*

The entrance to interim places takes you across four kinds of terrain. Each has its own challenge, its own brand of fear, and its own gift not available anywhere else. Each terrain feels so hazardous because of its barrenness, its suffocating density, and the depth of its penetration into the whole of your being. Use this information as a guide and know this: there is a way through each of the terrains of No Light, All is Lost, No End in Sight and No Escape.

# Cutting Up An Ox

*When I first began*
*I would see the whole ox before me*
*All in one mass.*
*But now, I see nothing with the eye.*
*My whole being apprehends.*
*My senses are idle. The spirit*
*Free to work without a plan*
*Follows its own instinct*
*Guided by natural line,*
*By the secret opening, the hidden space,*
*My cleaver finds its own way. . .*
*I cut through no joint, chop no bone.*
*There are spaces in the joints;*
*The blade is thin and keen.*
*When this thinness*
*Finds that space*
*There is all the room you need.*

—Chuang-Tzu [1]

### CHAPTER 3

## No Light
Your path disappears and a door opens

YOUR entry into interim places exposes you to inner terror unlike any fear you have ever known. The strange furnace is fueled by shifting circumstances coupled with a strong fear that can immobilize you. Your capacity to see and to know what to do with what you see are rendered useless.

My entry into interim places took place over several months. Clients canceled work dates. The phone stopped ringing. New clients never surfaced. Current clients stopped asking for more work. Satisfactory work results failed to generate word-of-mouth referrals. Bills began to mount. Compounding this, after my divorce, I supported two households. I became so completely terrified. I had always called upon God to help me in financially tight times before, and had witnessed miraculous changes. Now, my cries seemed to bounce off the sky. Only silence returned. And more fear.

You are tempted to work harder and longer, to expend maximum effort because it is what you know how to do. All of this energy is spent to no avail. You can see no way through. You have entered the land of No Light.

If this inner terrain were a real land mass that you could see and walk through, it would be a vast desert with no beginning or end. One day you find yourself there—no sand dunes, no mountains or wind-swept valleys. No features at all. You would be unable to discern where the land ends and the sky begins. You would immediately look for the path out but your apparent path in would have vanished completely. You would not know where you are, how far you had come, how far away you were from safety, or into what direction you should move. Complete disorientation.

Yes, this is the place called "lost."

Everywhere you look, everything has the same brown, barren look. You feel hot here; very small, and frightened by the absolute absence of anything that supports life. Your life, in particular.

This terrain of No Light left a bad taste in my body, not just my mouth, and the taste was the taste of my imminent death. All your worst emotional enemies live in No Light. If you fear financial ruin in your life, then you face the fear of utter ruin in No Light. If loneliness had been your enemy, then you wander around in the dark alone, looking for anyone or anything to save you and find no one or nothing. One morning you awake in this terrain and know that you have become prey for some powerful, invisible predator whom you didn't know but who seems to know you very well. This so-called predator is your sacred self.

No Light is a very real landscape.

No Light experiences baffle and terrify us. We don't know why they come, and we don't know which way to go. We can see nothing. German poet Rainier Rilke[2] once wrote about such experiences:

*It's possible I am pushing through solid rock*
*in flint-like layers as the ore lies alone.*
*I'm such a long way in I see no way through*
*and no space: everything is close to my face*
*and everything close to my face is stone.*
*I don't have much knowledge yet in grief*

*so this massive darkness makes me small.*
*You be the master,*
*make yourself fierce and break in*
*then my great grief cry will happen to you*
*and your great transforming will happen to me.*

The most difficult thing for you to do during your travels through the No Light terrain is acknowledge you simply cannot not see and do not know what to do. Behind your fear is a sense of powerlessness. The No Light terrain fills you with much bitterness and anger aimed everywhere—at yourself, at God, at all who refuse to give you your life on your terms.

Often your first clue that you have entered an interim place is your realization you are in this solitary darkness, a void where you learn you no longer get your life as you want it, when or how you want it. Your collective light cannot brighten this part of the path. We each must turn, like the great poet Rainier Rilke did, to another whose light we don't see, yet must learn to trust. No Light experiences are transformative moments, wherein we learn to stand still in the utter darkness, to breath deeply, to listen, and to move with each subtle move of the sacred within. Or we go crazy.

I went crazy first.

The more scared you feel, the more action you want to take. My experience was such that I couldn't quiet my head or the noise of all the old voices shouting their advice to me:

*Market more.*
*Make more phone calls.*
*Work harder.*
*Try harder.*
*Push more.*
*Stay busy, and keep moving.*
*Start again, and do all of this again but harder.*

I listened to my voices of experience and did everything they asked. Nothing worked. No one returned my phone calls or replied to my letters. Meetings that seemed to go well yielded no new work. For this child of alcoholism, my facade of controlling life through being successful and appearing to have things together was coming apart. I felt like I was dying—and should die. You may have this feeling too. What right to this life do people as lost and confused as us have? You begin to feel ugly and worthless, without value in a culture that places such a premium on smiles, success, and the semblance of constant forward movement and upward, expansive growth.

You want to die, or at least disappear from the face of the planet.

Some nights you may go to bed terrified at what you imagine will soon happen to you. You can easily see financial ruin and public shame consuming you. You have absolutely no insight on how you will manage to stay afloat or stay alive, let alone what you must do differently to achieve different results. This may be the first time in your life where you feel utterly lost and abandoned, shipwrecked on a planet where you no longer belong or deserve to live. When you wake in the morning, you may actually feel surprised you're still alive and wonder how this has happened. Your anguish is this strong.

In this part of the path, you feel terribly alone.

There are hidden times, however, that you must find. Times when you can quiet your mind and settle into the present moment. Notice how your mind seems to rest only when looking at things that are "Not You!" Things near, large or small, but important. While your strategic mind plots its survival and is convinced you will die, beneath this terror is a mysterious calmness. There is a tender place in your heart that remains relaxed and alert in the solitude and darkness of the No Light experience.

In this secret place, I knew I was safe, even though all was falling apart around me. I discovered that I felt wild and alive, even though my knees trembled and I honestly did not know how I would make ends meet. This place of quiet strength is with you, too, and always has been.

## ☽ *Secret openings, hidden doorways: recognizing the signposts*

➤ REMEMBER, WHEN YOU'RE IN CRISIS THERE ARE ALWAYS TWO COMPONENTS: the external world that is falling apart and your internal thoughts, feelings and assumptions. When you shift the internal, the external changes too. Focus inwardly and get clear about how you want to be in this time.

➤ THE ENDLESS NOISE IN YOUR MIND IS ACTUALLY AN OPENING, A HIDDEN DOORWAY TO SPIRIT. Therefore, find ways during each day or every other day to be alone. Alone in nature is even better. Pay attention to concrete, tangible things, i.e., the sound of the wind through the leaves; the way sparrows hustle about making love every few minutes in the air, on your fence post or anywhere; the way an afternoon sun softens the look and feel of pavement and glass; how old and memory-filled the smell of freshly cut grass is to you, the sound lake ice makes when it cracks, etc. Focus on something other than yourself and notice how all things go on with their life even while yours seems to be crashing to a halt.

➤ THE ABSENCE OF GRATITUDE, A TENDENCY TOWARDS BITTERNESS AND FRUSTRATION IS A SECRET OPENING. Give thanks for all of this even though you may not feel grateful.

➤ SHORTNESS OF BREATH. Find a few minutes each day to breathe deeply. When you're afraid, your breathing becomes shallow and insufficient. So does your thinking! Either at the start of each day or at the end, breathe deeply. Allow your thoughts to come and go as they do; focus on none of them. Just breathe.

➤ GIVE THANKS FOR THE ABILITY TO TAKE A BREATH. Bottom line, it means you're still alive at this moment. You're actually changing the way you stand in relationship with trauma, change and transition. Instead of getting caught up in the whirlwind drama, your work is to slow down, pay attention to what is going on immediately in and around you. And let this be enough.

Each of these activities involve recognizing hidden moments in each day when your spirit whispers, "Take a breath . . . look at the cloud patterns as they fall across and cast shadows on the hills to the north . . ." Hidden moments break the cycle of fear you are in and interrupt your preoccupation with fear. If only for a moment, there are opportunities that allow a sliver of light in.

## ❱ *When help is helpful and when it isn't*

My new love relationship was already a year old, and I felt comforted knowing Lisa was able to stand with me in these places. She lived a thousand miles away, but we remained connected through letters and telephone calls. Her love was grounding and, perhaps more than anything, allowed me to venture into these waters of the soul more deeply than I would have had the courage to do, had I been completely without companionship. To her great credit, Lisa encouraged me most by not trying to talk me out of my experience or my reactions to it. She stood by me and allowed me to have my experience without becoming overly terrified herself. I had space to struggle without my state requiring something from her other than her love, which she freely offered. Four years later, we would marry.

Help that is helpful allows you the dignity to have your struggle and hardship without it having to mean something about those closest to you. They cannot save you and the best they can offer is the space, the loving connection and the trust that you will find your own way through. The worst kind of "help" is the positive thinking slap on the back and encouragement to snap out of it, suck it up and just believe things will be okay. This kind of response, usually offered when your feelings make others feel uncomfortable, is of no use to you. Avoid others who are tempted to offer you quick advice on how to get out of your predicament. Sometimes, you can move through difficulty quickly with the right advice. Other times, transformation hits you on a much deeper level and impacts your identity and how you have organized yourself in this life. No quick fixes here, but the hidden openings and your sacred self will guide you.

In the tender, secret place of No Light, you can know and feel loved by a power beyond your own, yet still be deeply connected to who you really are. It was this same power that called you into interim places, as my own sacred self did with the promise of a deep shift in my life and work. This premonition lodged inside me the year before my marriage fell apart and two years before the significant downturn in my business. Upon reflection, you too, may recall feeling or being shown the possibility of another kind of life, sourced from a deeper place within. In No Light, however, you feel completely blind and ignorant about how to respond to what is happening.

No Light times rid us of the strategizing and controlling parts of our being. Jesus told his disciples, "Whoever loves and holds onto his life will lose it; whoever loses his life for my sake will find it." I came to know that He meant losing the part of us that wants to control and grasp our lives. All these years I thought these parts were my life! To lose them meant death. Looking everywhere, trying everything, we slowly begin to turn inward. Sometimes in despair and depression, but mostly because we know this is a time to draw aside and be alone. When you quiet yourself, you know with certainty that this is a time and place you cannot control, and you face forces with which you cannot negotiate. You must acknowledge this as truthfully as you can. "Yes, I have cancer . . . yes, my finances are gone . . . yes, my family member is addicted . . . yes, I feel lost and do not know what to do in this moment . . ."

When you acknowledge what you're up against, a very strange thing happens: you begin to feel strangely more alive than you have been in a long time! Your interim place, however, has many more challenging terrains in store for you. Yet opening to the experience you're actually having is a significant and courageous step.

# ❯ *The Sacred Self observes*

*Dearest brother in the light. We speak deliberately to you as a partner with us "in light" even though your experience now is of a complete absence of light. You seek clarity about what to do next to move from this place of pain, yet your seeking brings nothing but silence from the world. If there were nothing for you to do, you would not need light in which to do it. Even the act of trying to do something small (like contacting an old business client for a referral) makes your feeling of helplessness and powerlessness stronger, does it not? Looking out into the world for a response adds to your suffering because right now the door back into your old life in the world is no longer open to you. There is nothing for you to do but to surrender to this reality.*

*Listen to the wisdom that comes to you when you are quiet: the strange sense of aliveness and vitality that is not connected to achievement or success or linked to financial accumulation. Your wisdom (your light) says this is the new life you seek and it springs spontaneously from within you when you are quiet and when you breathe deeply from the center of your being. It is a hard thing for you to breathe this deeply when gripped by fear, but if you desire to do something, we say: "Quiet yourself regularly and breathe deeply and allow your essential life to spring forth."*

*This time is for you. Rest, be gentle with yourself. Allow the warrior in you who knows when to be quiet and still and when to move decisively to emerge. True prosperity and power are hidden in the heart, the last place humans look. Abundance on all levels originates here, is supplied here, is sustained here and received here. The challenge for you is to see the doorways in more clearly. Things are not always as they appear. Let's move in unison.*

*Know that we love you.*

## ☽ *Tools for the Journey*

**What to do when you're in No Light:**

➤ Trust your inner voice of the heart. It has night vision and works intuitively by knowing the next step you should take. In the absence of having a clear plan in your head, the intuitive wisdom of the heart often knows what to do, but only for now. In this moment.

➤ Become quiet, inquire and wait.

➤ Watch for serendipitous signs, chance run-ins with colleagues and friends, TV and media events that seem to grab your attention. Celebrate when they occur; do not concern yourself when they don't.

➤ Assume you are in the right place at the right time. All that is yours will come to you.

➤ Be open to moving in ways that may feel new and different.

A short note on experimenting with behaviors that feel new and different: When my business began to fall apart I "knew" I needed to paint pictures, even though I had never painted before! I still worked hard to stay afloat but I also began to paint. Sounds crazy. It was a simple, private action I could do with no one knowing about it. I filled my home with my work and Lisa's home as well. This quiet act made it easier to follow my inner direction months later when the sacred self asked for a more courageous, public response: writing this book. Just as crazy as painting. I had been schooled in private so when the public lessons began I was prepared. Watch for intuitive promptings in your own life and experiment by following them and keeping a record of what happens.

# The Question

*What was your vision of God's presence?*
*God's presence is there in front of me, a fire on the left,*
*A lovely stream on the right.*
*One group walks toward the fire, into the fire, another*
*Toward the sweet flowing water.*
*No one knows which are blessed and which not.*
*Whoever walks into the fire appears suddenly in the stream.*
*A head goes under on the water surface, that head*
*Pokes out of the fire.*
*Most people guard against going into the fire,*
*And so end up in it...*
*If you are a friend of God, fire is your water.*

*One molecule-mote-second thinking of God's reversal of comfort*
*And pain*
*Is better than any attending ritual. That splinter*
*Of intelligence is substance.*
*The fire and water themselves:*
*Accidental, done with mirrors.*

— Rumi [1]

### CHAPTER 4

# All is Lost

The humbling acknowledgement:
much of what we see is illusion.

THE All Is Lost terrain brings with it a deep despair of life itself. You may have been able to rely on your faith in God when hard times struck in the past. Now, the stakes feel higher. There seems more to lose. When you feel stress around big issues—money, health, physical safety, work/career and relationships, your mind sees only one thing: catastrophe. After falling back on old, overused strategies to no avail, circumstances now may be getting worse, not better. If you subscribe to the notion that there are no accidents, you must conclude that something significant is happening to you now, even though you feel cast adrift in a life-threatening river with a current faster than anything you have ever imagined. The deeper work in this terrain is to begin acquainting yourself with illusion, with how much fear is generated by what you believe is happening. You feel like you are being consumed by a fire; in truth, you are held in the water of spirit.

As my savings account dwindled and no work materialized, I felt all was lost. Money, busy work calendars, projects, ringing phones, full plates of engagements—I used all of this solid stuff of my life to confirm my existence, to shape how I saw myself as a man. I thought these things were me. When they disappeared, I felt I had disappeared. Or should have. I felt I had no right to be on earth when all that I mistook for me was gone.

When threatened or removed, certain elements that you hold dear to your very life reveal the deep cliff faces and drowning waters of All Is Lost, such as:

➤ Career setbacks, i.e., job loss, promotion denied, severe loss of income, new boss, expanded scope of responsibilities for which we are not well suited, significant reorganization resulting in loss of familiar support and recognition and opportunity for achievement.

➤ A financially viable future is suddenly lost through divorce, death, bad investments, unexpected illness or disability, etc.

➤ The loss of a child or partner.

➤ The loss of a part of our bodies or an important ability that springs from a healthy body though illness, disability, or injury.

➤ The subtle but painful loss of hope that accompanies depression. Its voice tells us our lives have no meaning now and never will. Depression is mysterious and seldom triggered by or connected to any tangible cause.

All Is Lost is often your body's deep response to the staggering recognition that something significant has happened and you no longer have control, power, or voice. If you ever did. I describe this terrain as a sheer cliff face or drowning waters in which no movement is safe or possible; even if it were, it would not be enough to save us. Remember, the poet Rilke[2] describes this experience as a tight, suffocating place which leaves us feeling very small:

*I'm such a long way in*
*I can see no way through and no space.*
*Everything is close to my face*
*and everything close to my face is stone.*
*I do not have much knowledge yet in grief*
*so this massive darkness*
*makes me feel small.*

The biblical character, Job, experienced the All Is Lost terrain in his life. In this story, God spoke with the devil. God boasts about how good a man Jacob is, while the devil responds that Job is only good because he has a lot of stuff. Take away the comforts, and Job would sing a different tune. God takes up the challenge and strips Job of everything. Nice bet.

The fact that the story ends well with Job being repaid threefold for all that he suffered affords me little comfort. Among his losses were his own family members. What is threefold payment for one child lost?

Your bitterness and resentment begin to build in All is Lost. I came to resent God for playing these silly games with people who, like me, thought their lives were important matters. Sometimes I think the universe needs a lesson in just what it really feels like to be human. And maybe we need a lesson in how the universe really works. The All is Lost experiences ambush you from out of nowhere. You feel bewildered by what is happening, angry and resentful at the apparent change in rules you thought you understood. Like the great poet, we do not have much knowledge yet in grief so this massive darkness makes us feel small.

Like Job, you search yourself to see if you have done something worthy of this, as if understanding "why" would help! Perhaps you notice small things. Yet, in interim places, you can see no shift in your life or work that would account for the drastic shift in the results you see now.

Unlike Job, your once-strong faith may begin to disappear as you grow more and more resentful towards God for allowing the life you have loved to slip away. Your grasp on your life tightens. All you can do is watch.

**Whose life is it, anyway?**

We stumble into the All Is Lost terrain when the plan we have for our life collides with the plan our true life has for us. What looks and feels like loss is actually a doorway into a new, as yet unexperienced life. Having a conceptual model of this brings no consolation; finding a way once again to quiet yourself and breathe deeply gives you brief glimpses of this that you know to be true. Knowing is stronger than believing; you know with your whole body and being while you believe only with your mind. It is only as you learn to quiet yourself through walking, sitting and breathing that you gain access to this quiet place of knowing within. This quiet knowing, made possible by stepping aside from the activity of your life and breathing deeply, carries within it the beginning seeds of discernment. Perhaps only for a minute or two each day, you can begin to know the difference between fire and water, between illusion and what's real.

## ❯ Secret openings, hidden doorways: recognizing the signposts

You have never felt so small as you do in this All Is Lost terrain. In my days of forced solitude, I worried about how and whether I would ever be able to recover the days, weeks, and months that I had lost. Moses wandering around in the desert for forty years sounds like an extravagant waste of time, yet a real fear when feeling that All is Lost. You worry:

"What if I never recover the lost ground, the lost money, the lost health, the lost years of my life's contribution? What about the children, the business, the retirement?"

Again, resentment is a telltale sign of something needing release. What are you holding onto?

Your sacred self's response to these questions may be stone silence. It feels like indifference, and indifference can sometimes be worse than rejection. When I was a young boy, my father, wrapped tightly in drunkenness and work-related absence, responded with indifference to me. To be greeted again by indifference felt both familiar and timely; the invitation to release an old wound and move on became clear.

Rilke[3] continues:

*I do not have much knowledge yet in grief*
*so this massive darkness makes me small.*
*You be the master, make yourself fierce*
*break in*
*Then my great grief cry will happen to you*
*and your great transforming will happen to me.*

As we travel through the All Is Lost terrain, what we want is an end to the suffering. What God offers is an exchange of our grief for His transforming us. That's the deal. We take it or leave it. Notice that while Rilke describes a place of formidable isolation and obstruction, he does not hurry to get out to more comfortable footing. Standing still, he is able to discern the presence of another: *"You be the master, make yourself fierce..."* You must begin here to acknowledge and surrender your grief— in the form of anger, fear, sadness over all that seems lost. This may require a solitary act of desperation, but this action is a secret, hidden way to confront bitterness and lay aside the feeling of powerlessness that has become so much a part of your everyday life. There is nothing etheric, lofty or even

spiritual about this decision; it is simply what a tired trav-
eler has to do.

Take the transaction Rilke describes, grief for transformation — slowly. Day by day.

As you surrender each day, you slowly begin to realize
that you have been adding to your suffering by imagining all
would be lost forever before actually losing anything. You
tell stories to yourself about how catastrophic everything
will surely become at some future point that is fast
approaching but never actually arrives. I told myself that the
divorce would destroy my relationship with my daughter,
Cate. It actually grew stronger as each of us individually did.
I told myself that financial ruin would destroy me, and it
would invariably bring me shame. Times, in fact, were tight,
but I have not gone down in ruin yet and whatever shame I
have endured has been internal and self-induced. You begin
to realize how lost in illusion you have become!

It would take a long time, but one day I just got tired of
my stories. I grew tired of listening to myself. I wanted to
live my life again, not by old strategies that made me small
but by life affirming strategies that come from within.
Listen in your quiet moments and you will hear all the old
stories repeated a thousand times and you will see how tired
you really are of the old noise.

All is Lost prepares you for transformation and the new
life you dream about but seldom talk about.

**The slow, boring work of dying and transformation**

Transforming is silent work, largely unknown and invisible to us. Much of this time you feel as if nothing good is
happening. Transformation is talked about in books and
management magazines yet is utterly devalued in our culture. So, you may naturally devalue it. It happens for reasons
that are mysterious to us. Know this for sure: while you are

in the All Is Lost terrain, an important part of you is dying and you grieve its passing. For me, it was the tightly clenched part of me that believed it knew what's best for me and my life. It knew what should happen, how it should happen, and when it should happen. It knew how I should spend my time and energy, and it knew what God should deem as important.

**I don't know anything now.**

Your essential work in All Is Lost terrain is personal transaction with the sacred: your grief cry for God's transforming. In some fundamental way, this terrain brings you to an end in your self. It is not a glamorous place where we appear on the cover of *Fortune* and our life's accomplishments are touted. You release your grip on ordered lives and replace them with trust that a new understanding of life, transfused into our consciousness by God, will at some point arrive. Until then, you hang out and allow the old way to die, as you might watch the moon disappear on the morning horizon. The dying may not be pretty or comfortable.

When I began to let go, however, I did not know about surrender or about what follows. I began to learn the disciplines of falling apart masterfully—faith and faithlessness, cowardice and courage—to allow my old ways to die and to allow and receive God's new ways as they emerged. *Masterfully*, in my awakened experience, means learning how to be present to and experience all of what happens within and around me. To deny or run away from nothing. To face everything. Dying to old ways is ragged, uncomfortable, simultaneously peaceful and bitterly upsetting . . . all at once.

To equate this kind of emotional upheaval with mastery of any sort may feel absurd. Definitions change, remember? You're in All is Lost. Lose the old definition of mastery, of what it means to have your life together. If you stand and experience this terrain you can do anything!

Some days, you will be full of fear or anger. Uncertainty may be a constant companion. Other days, you will feel quite bored and will see this time as an irrelevant, senseless waste of time. You will feel forgotten and left behind. Still, there will be moments of certain clarity where you will know that you are being rearranged, rebuilt from the inside out by a master craftsperson. These are typical feelings of All is Lost.

It would be many months before I concluded that all is never lost in an interim place. Never. Our bodies receive the full experience of our life here, the joys as well as the suffering. Everything else is held for us in love until another time.

All of your great plans and ideas, your brilliant strategies and notions about how things should work are very fragile even though you act as if they are cast in granite. When your great plan falls apart all you are left with is bewilderment, anger and fear. It is as if the universe, sensing your desire to move forward, strips you of that which is prized and, while you are without it, opens you in a deeper way to live, to work, heal, build or rest. This mysterious blade then brings to the surface your true giftedness and beauty, your desire to serve and live fully. In some cases, you then are given back what you originally wanted, only now you are changed. You can receive it as if for the first time and move into the world in a very different, less attached, way. The grasp you have on your life, and the circumstances and people in it, slowly begins to loosen.

Again, as this deep work happens in you, you are often aware of nothing except your own anguish, or boredom and separation from everything that matters.

Sometimes, you don't get back what you once thought was yours. A loved one dies. An opportunity is lost and does not return. Your cry of grief lasts longer and stays partially lodged in your bones where your voice and tears cannot find it. In this way you are also changed. Your life doesn't meet you on your own terms but reminds you, in its own mysterious way, there is a deeper current that is beyond all analysis, beyond all categories and descriptive small boxes, and is more magnificently complex than any self help books can comprehend. You reluctantly bow and accept your own mystery.

Interim places reveal the mystical connection between us and the universe, whose ways we never fully know. Yet, a tender, very shy place in the heart knows this and, alone, can rest safely in the arms of the unknown. This tender place enters on the long, deep breath you breathe this moment. It exists now, in this moment only, within you. It can't be found any other way.

I have spent so much time looking.

# ❯ *The Sacred Self observes*

*Our partner, our beloved and beautiful partner, you have done all that was necessary to arrive at this moment. In earlier times, you might have chosen to continue on the path into the world and you might have done well. It was not time for you to know of a different way. There is no judgment here, only this reminder: you knew there was a better way, a different way, a path that led to partnership with the "US" that is God within you. This is why you wept when you read accounts of people who live simply, in harmony with the universe and have all of their needs supplied daily. This is why you felt so alive during similar times yourself and why all work you do that does not have a sacred core message in it leaves you unsatisfied. And it is this yearning to know and then to teach about sacred partnership that has led you to this experience of being lost in your own life.*

*The end of ego-driven power is where the spiritual life and power often begins. You have been experiencing a death to certain ways of being in the world that have served you well for many years. This time of unbidden solitude is not punishment but rather an invitation to new life. None of this matters right now. Parts of you are dying, and there is little more than fear and grief as these aspects leave you. We have said to you (unmistakably and clearly in ways you knew came from us) that you are safe and would be safe even though your fear of financial ruin was strong. We have whispered ways through impossible passageways that helped you on your way. We love you, dearest one, and are greatly honored to serve you and speak with you and be in deeper relationship with you. We will never leave you nor will we ever leave you without encouragement.*

*In every great project or endeavor, be it a family, a job, a project, a relationship or a book, there is a crossroads reached where the original vision or joy is lost, hopelessly thwarted by obstacles, delays, and obstructions. There is much fear in this place. It is at this point that people often revert to old ways that have brought them success and comfort in the past. There are three core strategies that are often invoked: (1) let go of the original vision and pursue something else with vigor, (2) let go of the original vision and stay engaged with activity but not emotionally committed to anything in particular . . . or (3) force the original vision to be achieved by willpower alone. These each have merit and are easily embraced in your culture. Yet there is another way that you already know about in your heart.*

*It is the way of surrender and relinquishment of desire to spirit, dearest one. It is only this way that brings the full resources and power within you and outside of you to bear on your circumstances. It is the one strategy that is most fiercely resisted by you and others, dearest one, because you are convinced you are separate from the divine, sepa-*

*rate from all that you desire, and even separate from the fire that sparks and sustains your life itself. In this illusion of separation, you grasp at life when you are under stress and the grasping itself brings more stress.*

*You are neither separate or alone, dearest one, but these words bring no comfort.*

*The surrender we speak of requires relinquishing your experience to spirit while remaining vigilant and attentive, anticipating a response. Sometimes this response comes quickly; sometimes not. Sometimes the path through your dilemma is what you thought it would be, but often it is not. Sometimes the solution brings relief and joy, yet sometimes there is sorrow and bewilderment. We will speak more of these things later. We wish to state clearly that the doorway to the sacred life within most always appears initially as something to be rejected. Interim places like these must be surrendered often, never rejected.*

## ❱ *Tools for the Journey*

**What to do in All is Lost:**

➤ Allow yourself space and time for grieving what has been lost. Anger is often a surface feeling hiding a deeper experience of fear and sadness. See if you can feel these, and then release them to God, as you understand him.

➤ Be especially gentle and compassionate with yourself; you are in terrain that many others avoid at all cost, and so bring added suffering to themselves and their families.

➤ Watch out for the tendency to imagine the worst catastrophes happening in the future and then fearing them now, as if they are the only possibility. When I come to this place with my fear of what the situation looks like, my sacred self says, "So it seems," as if it knows what is truly going on. (See more in Chapter 3.) Example: My assessment might be to say, "This project is coming apart at the seams!" To which the sacred self replies, "So it seems." I've learned there's much going on that we do not see! This marks a subtle but important shift in your life even though many do not recognize it as such. You are being shown how to stand in the center of your own life, acknowledge it fully, yet remain unattached to it all and open for what wants to happen next. "So it seems" is a powerful, understated way of being in relationship to suffering . . . in a different way!

➤ Remember, that no matter how difficult the circumstances, you are still the one having the experience, the one who can sit back and watch it all happening and give names to what is seen and felt. This makes you separate from and stronger than the experience.

➤ In quieter moments, ask for assistance finding the part of you which is unafraid. Expect a response. Remember, you've made it this far. There is a part of you that knows what is needed.

➤ Release difficult circumstances to God, as you understand him. Keep notes about what transpires.

Your challenges may be far from over. As this part of your life unfolds, weeks can become months and the emotional landscape poses new threats and challenges. Your travels are about to yield even greater gifts.

# It Has Not Rained Light Here

*It has not rained light for many days.*
*The wells in most eyes look*
*Drought-stricken . . .*
*Everyone has become ill*
*From guarding*
*Nothing.*
*Careers and cities can appear real in this*
*Intense*
*Desert heat.*
*But I say to my close ones,*
*"Don't get lost in them,*
*It has not rained light there for days.*
*Look, most everyone is diseased*
*From 'making love' to*
*Nothing."*

—Hafiz[1]

### CHAPTER 5

# No End in Sight
## The art and practice of not looking

MUCH of the pain I experienced in interim places I brought upon myself without knowing it at the time. Guarding and making love to nothing. You can help yourself by becoming familiar with the emotional terrain of this time in your life. Somehow, it helps you gain distance from the experience by naming different aspects of it. This next terrain is the most difficult because, as the name suggests, it feels like it will go on forever.

Interim places leave you feeling there'll be no end to your suffering. You wish for an immediate end, hope for a magic pill to ease your aches, or pray for divine intervention to instantly turn everything your way, only to realize these only add to your torment. You may spend considerable energy avoiding this place in the journey because it is frightening, very lonely, and emasculating. After all, what weakling (I argued to myself) gets himself into situations where there is no end in sight? And no way to escape.

Even God seems weak and without power in this terrain. When you imagine yourself in darkness, the whole world seems dark.

As you move through the No End In Sight terrain, you look endlessly at the horizon of your fragile life — desperate for assistance, for change, for hope, or for deliverance. You find nothing, see nothing, hear nothing and receive nothing. All synchronicity disappears and everything feels hard, *" . . . everything was close to my face, and everything close to my face was stone.²"* In No End In Sight terrain, catastrophe feels certain while the sense of direction and purpose you long for feels far away. All action seems a waste of time and you convince yourself the sum total of your action and your very presence on the planet have amounted to absolutely nothing at all.

No End In Sight is a landscape of illusion. What feels like a waste of time (gentleness with and opening to yourself, curiosity and risk taking) is actually very significant and what feels significant (all action taken in fear) is often a waste of time.

You feel a combination of disorientation and fear for many days, weeks or months before you realize there is an additional feeling hidden within your fear: the subtlest, sweetest curiosity and wonder you have ever known. Experiences like the one that follows aided me in becoming more curious about what was really going on in my life. And made me feel less fearful.

One day I went out for a jog, where I do some of my best reflecting. I felt worried about the lack of work and income and could see no end to the downturn. Suddenly, from deep within my heart, a voice simply asked this question: *What if you are perfectly safe as you are?*

I felt immediately elated by the loving power and clarity of this voice and knew it was an important moment to take note of. I immediately saw that I had been so focused on worrying about the future that I had forgotten that I was actually alive right now. I was having an experience right now on this run that was good and wonderful in its own right. I began slowly to recognize that all I had ever been afraid of in my life were negative images of my future. Most of what I feared had never actually happened! Yet I had missed much of my life while I fretted about the future.

I recognized this as my *sacred self* speaking directly to me. Sometimes you simply know what you've experienced. I felt instant remembrance and spontaneous freedom. I felt hopeful at even the possibility that my life was not as bleak as I imagined it to be. I felt free to consider the possibility that *all was not as it appeared.* I was not yet able to see or sustain a positive expectation about this but the momentary crack in my dense view of reality drew light into me. And a glimmer of freedom.

I began to see that I was in a battle between my head (which constantly strategizes for ways to remain safe, in control and on top of things) and my heart (which simply knows what is best and highest for me and often knows what to do). Yet this jogging experience revealed another dimension to me: the presence of another, deeper and clearer voice within that was beyond my head and heart, my ego and my personality, beyond my fear and my hope, yet intimately familiar with all of me. In previous chapters I have called this aspect of me my "sacred self." I met it in the No End in Sight terrain.

I have struggled to name this part of me accurately and feel only marginally satisfied with my current wording. Some people refer to their higher self in ways that are similar to what I describe as the sacred self. Higher connotes above or better than, neither of which has been my experience of the sacred self. Sometimes, higher self suggests the highest or best part of my personality, which I also reject. The sacred self seems open and loving towards all of me, the good and bad. Sacred unfortunately suggests a religious connection which I regret, since nothing I experience with the sacred self implies any religious affiliation. There is, instead, a deep, unified connection with God, Spirit, the Universal Source or whatever words describe the overwhelming conscious love energy with which our universe is constructed and held together. It is my experience with this deeply aligned, love presence within, that I ascribe the word "sacred" to.

Your sacred self has a unique focus in the terrain of interim places. It seeks to illuminate the illusion that keeps your head stuck in fear while speaking clearly and gently to the heart about the need to open more fully to all experience. Sometimes, it speaks with words and brings instant clarity to a situation, as it did in my run. You immediately see the illusion you had mistaken for your future, and are opened to the possibility that there could be many realities in the future, not just the one you feared. Other times, the sacred self influences situations, brings about coincidences or orchestrates circumstances to bring about resolution to choices we have made. Always, though in ways you seldom understand in the moment, the sacred self works for your highest good.

## ❯ *Secret openings, hidden doorways: recognizing the signposts*

Navigating the terrains in your interim place brings you to a point in your journey where you rightfully wonder— 'How much of my life is real? How much of what I think I see happening in my life is real? Do circumstances cause fear in me or do I cause fear in me? How much of my fear is connected to what is objectively happening? How much is triggered by my imagination? Is constant activity, incessant busyness and motion the best response to deeper questions about my life? Or yet another reaction to my fear?' These questions, if they are yours, reveal secret openings to another way of being in relationship with your own life and with this trauma in particular. You shape a new future by asking new questions. In No End in Sight, your questions begin to change. See them as prompts from your sacred self.

The sacred self speaks with spontaneous clarity, and even people as dense as you and me can occasionally hear its voice. You slowly learn that you don't need to do anything other than cultivate the quiet place of the heart within. You may have to fight your instinctive reaction to this terrain, i.e., to do something, anything, as long as you keep moving. (I am, after all, a high-achieving workaholic, son of an alcoholic. *Doing things* is who I am.) Cultivating a quiet, open heart, however, is the hardest work of all because you must see through illusion, a topic I will write more about in the next section. Illusion feels real. As real as Rilke's *"solid rock close to the face."* That's what makes it so difficult to see through.

You slowly come to see that you do in fact have options when you look out at a bleak future and see no end in sight to your troubles. First, you can work harder and longer to force the future you want through will power alone. This strategy essentially keeps you doing the same things that brought you to this place, only harder and with greater determination. Most people and organizations choose this strategy and build it into their corporate cultures, like I did.

It is an exhausting option but one that sometimes works. More frequently, however, it fails because nothing has changed. You think the same way you have always thought and behave the same way you have always behaved. Yet, you're expecting different results. Someone once wrote that this is the working definition *crazy.*

Another strategy is to stop looking at the future and devote all your energy to fixing the present. Here, the frenetic energy is diverted into problem solving and crisis management but without the desire. A vision might have been instilled had it been present. Fixing the present is a popular strategy because it holds the promise of endless activity and the illusion of movement, both very important deceptions to most of us. I have lived with this strategy for a long time. If I could have just stayed busy, if the phones had kept ringing with more work and more travel, I might still be immersed in it. I feel like a "real man" when I am on the go and doing many things all at once. Endless busyness is seductive to me and you might get caught up in it too.

It is entirely possible for you to be very busy and yet stray a long way from the life you came here to live. I know this now. It is possible to have days filled with activity but to be in the wrong days altogether. It is possible to have a full plate of engagements, while the heart starves for the vitality and nourishment it still needs. It is possible that when the bottom falls out of your dry and busy days, when all hope is gone and there is no end in sight, that this moment is the exact and perfect moment the sacred self has orchestrated for its own mysterious purpose. Your exhaustion with the act of looking itself is a hidden opening given you by your sacred self.

It is possible that when the future you see seems too harsh to consider, one powerful option is to stop considering it at all.

Your challenge in No End in Sight is to turn and face yourself and your life as it is today, in this present moment. Slowly, you face your loneliness and your fear. You stop running from your experience and begin just to feel it. I wrote about it. I began to discover that loneliness and fear were only part of my whole experience of living. Not the whole thing. In any one day I could feel happy, sad, confused, very clear, productive, and creative. I also discovered that none of what I experienced was me. My actual self, the essence of who I really am, my sacred self, seemed to watch all of my feelings with loving detachment. It is as if there is a place inside the heart that says to me: "I am more than all my experience and greater than the sum of all my feelings."

And you are too.

# ❯ *Befriending our fear, finding our true capacity*

No End in Sight invites you to befriend your fears. All of what you need to learn is contained in your present experience, the last place you normally look. You have already acknowledged the truth about the circumstances you are in. You have surrendered your grief. Now, your task is to daily slip beneath the surface emotions and touch the deeper core of your experience. You are the owner of an extraordinary guesthouse called your life; welcome the fear and confusion. Strike up a conversation. Befriending them opens a doorway into the future you desire.

Upon reflection, you begin to see that what you actually fear is the lack of capacity to experience and handle your own life. I strived to control things through achievement, respect of people I admired and accumulating financial reserves because I wasn't sure I could live if I didn't do these things! Even my imagining negative futures is an attempt to control that which is beyond control. When all the known landmarks of our identity—achievement, work, financial well-being, and a sense of belongingness to our friends, our organization, our children, and partners—are stripped away, what do we hold onto? Or do we have to hold onto anything at all? We fear not being able to withstand this experience.

In light of this fear, challenge yourself to slow down and breathe each day, a simple sounding plan that some days requires nothing short of a singular act of courage. That I am sitting here writing about this is a testimony to my capacity, since to be a witness to my experience makes me greater than, and more powerful than my experience. It is, after all, while learning to rest in the present that you discover (and continue to discover) the presence and resourcefulness of the sacred self. It lays just on the other side of your fear.

**When you build credible evidence of your sacred self, your own capacity to creatively respond to your life increases!**

No End in Sight points you in the direction of home. You are beginning to see the fruits of early surrender, inviting spirit to come into your days and recording what then happens.

## ❭ *The Sacred Self observes*

*Our dearest brother in the light. We bring you love and light and are honored to join you in these pages and to speak as friends about standing in the midst of your life without shrinking back or seeking an escape. How can you escape from yourself? These days are hard for you and very lonely. You speak of separation and isolation, both old friends of yours and they are a wound that never quite heals in your heart. Is this not so? You speak also of these open spaces as being both terrifying and healing; it is true. The terror comes from two errors in thinking and a third error in right relationship.*

*The first troublesome assumption in thinking is that a change in circumstance is a long way off in time, i.e., no end in sight. Part of what makes your human experience so mysterious and exciting is that change can come upon you suddenly, without warning, and completely disrupt everything. A chance meeting, a single phone call with good news or bad, a project that turns out unexpectedly great or poor, news from a doctor, a lawyer, a stock broker, a loved one can suddenly turn a life in a completely new direction. You see no end in sight; we say to you, things can change in an instant and all that has been lost can be restored overnight. All things are, indeed, possible. Is this not the message of your great religious teachers and prophets?*

*A second aspect of your thinking is related to the first.*

*It has to do with the assumption that you are alone, separate and without resources. There are countless events in your human experience that can easily trigger the feeling of separation. The actual reality is that even God, as you define God, is unable to create isolation and separation from His creation. On this side, we know only loving union with all, which includes loving union with you. It is not possible for us to become separate from you because the loving union is the substance that binds all creation! We are unable to take our eyes off of you, you are that beautiful and precious!*

*The assumption of separation is an illusion that creates anger and fear. Let go of it. When you are in situations that evoke the feeling of separation, be open to this experience and then let it go as well. But do not fight your own experience; rather, be in right relationship to it.*

*When we speak of being in right relationship with your hardship we say that you can know with certainty that all things that come into your life pass through our hands first. And all things are for your highest good, even though this is hard to fathom at times. We say there are no accidents, no feelings or experiences that are not part of the plan that you and we created for your life and continue to refine as we move forward.*

*The full creative power of the universe is available to the one who is quiet and grounded in the truth of what we have just said to you. Choices made in fear carry little long lasting significance and often create great damage. Choices made from a stance of union and love carry profound significance and harness the power of the full human spirit— yours and ours together—fullness.*

*Even now, you are able to stand in the midst of great turmoil and breathe in deeply the present moment. You are able to see and appreciate that in this moment right now you are enough and you have all that you require to move into the next moment. Nothing else matters. In the days ahead, the spoken intention that comes out of your mouth from this stance of quiet rest and confidence will carry great power. All that seems hard now will become easy then. Let these words comfort you tonight. And, as always, know that we love you and are honored by your desire to speak with us.*

## ☽ Tools for the Journey

### What to do through No End in Sight:

➤ Stop looking for an end. If it hasn't happened yet, it is not real yet! Take comfort in this.

➤ Know with certainty that you're not seeing the future but only your imagination of what it might be.

➤ Start looking at your present reality. Today, this moment, right now, your actual life, the one happening right now where you are. Are you safe now? Do you have food and warmth? Are those you care for safe and healthy? Do you have money for what you need now, this afternoon? Can you draw a deep breath now?

➤ Are there things to be thankful for today? What are they? List them.

➤ Express your gratefulness for this moment: for your breath, your clothing, your food and other items so basic to your survival that you take them for granted. Gratefulness matters. It changes you and a different you may be able to change other things.

➤ Choose a day or portion of a day and do something that brings you joy. See this as a way to make a statement about the future you desire: I will no longer delay my joy, freedom and peace until conditions are right . . . I choose these qualities now.

➤  Again, surrender or release all views of the future: all that you fear has been lost, and all you fear the future will bring you. Invite the universe into the very midst of the catastrophe.

➤  Keep a journal or notes of what happens.

In the secret place of the heart you may know you are still running, still attempting to make something happen in your life. For all the right reasons (family obligations, health, safety, career advancement, etc.) you continue to attempt to exercise control over circumstances that are clearly beyond your influence. Your prayers still contain conditions and specific instructions and how to strategize for God. In real ways, you still delay your happiness until some lasting conditions are changed in yourself, in other people or in the circumstances. You, still, continue to grasp your life too tightly to actually enjoy yourself.

There is one more terrain that will bring an end to your struggling and maneuvering.

*We already have everything we need.*

—Pema Chodrön

### CHAPTER 6

# No Escape
Losing control and finding life

BUDDHIST author Pema Chodrön, in *Start Where You Are: A Guide to Compassionate Living*[1] says that we live in a universe in which we do not need to hide from ourselves and run from who we are. We don't need fixing. And we don't need to run away and escape. Our life finds us out. We may escape for a while, but sooner or later, our life serves up the same old issues we tried running from and invites us to look at them again. There is no escape. This news comes as a threatening surprise to those like me who want to control the show.

No Escape requires that you stop running. You come to an end. You realize the end is in yourself. The art in this movement is to face your life as you are *but without attempting to fix anything*. The heart does not want to be fixed; it just wants you to know it and know it fully.

We Americans are fascinated with negativity and fixing what is perceived as wrong. We have virtually no interest, strangely enough, in exploring and understanding the darker parts of the human condition. We want to run from it, just fix it and make it go away. In my twenty years in leadership development, I discovered that workshop participants tend to fall into two categories: those who were sent to be fixed and those who chose voluntarily to attend, hoping they would be fixed quickly and made better. Most of my own personal change efforts have amounted to nothing more than cleverly disguised strategies to keep me from facing myself—as if there was something permanently wrong or innately "less than" about me.

This view almost cost me my life. I disregarded even the most valid, clearly communicated feedback if it felt dangerously close to the "less than" feelings within me, which I had subconsciously adopted as the *truth* about me. Interim places bring us face to face with our real games of escape we've played with ourselves for a long time.

You learn in No Escape that all strategies which have *fixing you* as their central goal fail because the soul doesn't need fixing. Strategies that help you avoid what's uncomfortable will ultimately fail because the soul demands that you grow. And growth requires leaning into the discomfort, the pain of the unknown.

Intelligent, successful, and well-adjusted people like you may ask: How could there be regions in me I don't know about or understand? How can the desire to change myself and grow actually keep me from growing? How is it that developmental action plans, part of good performance evaluation systems, actually keep people from flourishing in their career?

Rilke[2] wrestled with such questions in an excerpt from "The Man Watching":

*What we choose to fight against is so tiny!*
*What fights us is so great!*
*. . . When we win its with small things,*
*and the triumph itself makes us small.*
*What is extraordinary and eternal*
*does not want to be bent by us.*
*. . . This is how he grows: by being defeated, decisively,*
*by constantly greater beings.*

This piece indicates that vital elements under the surface will resist and must resist your efforts to change them. Your deeper longings and desire, your destiny and sense of purpose, and the fear of embracing these essential aspects of yourself may lie far below the surface of your public behavior. Your small attempts to fix yourself amount to nothing but diversions that keep you from wading into deeper waters. What is *extraordinary and eternal* in us refuses to be bent by us. As I have written earlier, my striving for success and respect by always staying active and busy actually kept me from learning how to quiet myself and receive wisdom and guidance from the truest part of me, my sacred self. Moreover, to turn and face this need for quietness within has felt nothing short of terrifying for me. You and I have been dragged into this unbidden terrain by our sacred self, a *greater being.* Rilke was too.

## ☽ *Secret openings, hidden doorways: recognizing the signposts*

The time you spend traveling in No Escape offers you sacred openings to the eternal sacred self within. It is a compassionate (and humorous) universe that cleverly devises a life path with no permanent escape route. The following subtle and not so subtle shifts are signs you have entered No Escape and indicates that your sacred self wants you to stop and reconsider who you think you are and what you're doing.

> ➤ DRUGS, SEX, WORKAHOLISM, SUPERFICIAL LIVING, MATERIALISM, AND ACTIVITY ADDICTIONS. Look for any shifts in your behavior. These behaviors may relieve anxiety for awhile, but your deeper life has already laid siege around you and simply wants you out. Like a medieval enemy

camped outside the city gate, your true life lies, waiting to ambush and call you back to the path that is yours alone. You know this is true when you quiet yourself.

➤ YOU FEEL EXHAUSTED FROM TRYING HARD TO FORCE CIR-CUMSTANCES TO CHANGE AND YOU'VE BECOME TIRED OF JUDGING YOURSELF. Again, exhaustion is always a secret opening, a hidden space not to do more but to stop. Now, in this sentence! You must embrace what you run from.

➤ YOU'RE FED UP WITH TRYING TO SEE THIS EPISODE AS A LEARNING EXPERIENCE! You no longer want to learn a damn thing. Forget about personal change. Instead, your challenge is to pursue a path of awareness and understanding, with compassion. Whatever truly must change will, with awareness. No cut or bruise needs to be talked into healing. The body is naturally inclined toward growth and wellness.

➤ NO ESCAPE FEELS LIKE A FINAL DEATH BLOW TO YOUR CON-TROL AGENDA. It is. Everything is perfect as it is, although parts may still remain a mystery. Understanding what's happening may satisfy your control needs, but letting go and moving forward, in the absence of understanding it all, brings you closer to your true destination. The exaggerated need to understand "why" is also an indicator from your sacred self that you're attempting to control your future by knowing more. Release the need to know and step into the flow of your life today. See what happens.

➤ PAY ATTENTION TO SHIFTS IN WHAT YOU DESIRE. The change and growth you honestly desire (because you know it serves the highest good of all concerned) are already happening. Or you would not want them. This requires faith. The new life originally takes shape in your heart (as tension, unrest, longing), then your mind (thoughts, ideas), then your voice, and finally, your behavior and experiences. In quiet moments, where you weep silently and peacefully without warning, you are likely glimpsing aspects of your desired future showing themselves to you.

➤ YOU BEGIN TO EXPERIENCE THE STRANGEST THING YOU'VE EVER FELT: compassion for yourself! Somehow, you have stumbled on the discovery that we are all magnificently flawed and perfectly ragged, contradictory and, nevertheless, completely human. Inwardly, you relax more deeply into this awareness. The media tells us we should all be thin and endlessly confident, always happy, always self-assured, drive shiny new cars, and continuously be stocked with lots of beer. Try to be serious!

Once your sacred self lets you experience turning to compassionately face yourself as you truly are, I am convinced that deep, imperceptible change begins to occur spontaneously in ways you cannot imagine. You move from a posture of despising yourself, your body, and your painful experiences and negative feelings to a posture of openness and acceptance of yourself. It does not mean you stop growing or changing. That is impossible. Every living thing changes. Rather, this shift means you stop trying to order your life to do what you think it should do. You begin to enter the deeper wellspring of living and allow the truest part of yourself to direct you. Interim places are designed to bring you to this moment!

As you stop running and hiding from yourself, something begins to shift in the secret places of your heart. You begin to sense, on the other side of fear, doubt and negativity, the presence of something new. A confidence in your true capacity. You find ways to get through. Solutions you have not known come along. Needed resources show up in surprising ways. Clarity about dilemmas comes just in time. I knew I was shifting when tears of gratitude washed over my soft and tired eyes. I began to rest more deeply and feel genuinely refreshed in the morning. I began to be grateful for small things, for the play of sunlight and shadow in the late afternoon, for sparrows tirelessly building their city of nests near the porch, for catching a glimpse of Lisa and staring at her beauty until she caught me looking.

In No Escape, you begin to allow what wants to happen to happen and you are spontaneously grateful for what develops. You become curious, again, and look at reality with a sense of wonder and even amusement, not as much terror. Reality is what it is—nothing more, nothing less.

Gratitude and compassion, coupled with a willingness to *simply acknowledge what is*, are signs of the presence of the sacred self. Signs that your relationship with yourself and your life are shifting. Know this now.

## ☽ *The Sacred Self observes*

*Dearest brother in the light, is it not strange to you that the most prized moment for us is the most despised moment for you? This is a point of some humor on this side of life that is seen very differently on earth. Let us explain. There is a deep surrender possible only when a person realizes there can be no escape. Prior to this surrender there is much fear, even terror and uncertainty, as you have known. Instead of seeing this as a time when the unlimited resources of the universe will finally be available, fear persuades you that you will finally be imprisoned for a life of scarcity, emptiness or hopelessness. The point where you are closest to breakthrough is often felt to be a time of cer-*

tain disaster. You have reached an impasse and can proceed no further.

You have come to an end of the road.

It is a road that no longer served you, however, and there is a new road that only now opens to you. This road opens through your surrender and is entered through your curiosity and wonder. The fuel for your journey here is gratitude and trust.

The surrender we speak of is the releasing of concern and desire into the arms of a powerful and loving partner who can do what you are no longer able to do. Curiosity and wonder fill the heart with expectancy but not about a distant future. The expectancy we speak of is centered in this moment; now, today. Not about the future. As you listen to or read these words now, you are alive. You have somehow made it this far. You have drawn a breath. You have needed to pause. These small acts are truly beautiful aspects of who you are, dearest one, and we honor you for your courage and tenacity and for the steadfastness of your integrity and commitment. Let your heart be filled with gratitude for we say to you that many people would not have the courage to simply pause and allow themselves the experience of having no escape possible for their lives. And so would miss the doorway we speak of now.

Much of your life, and the lives of others, is spent doing things you hope will bring fullness, meaning and possessions into your life. In this pursuit, you attempt to bring what is "out there and far away" into your experience. This is simply the way of things in your culture. There is no judgment here. But the pursuit itself creates separation and loneliness; you are frequently left on the outside of your own life, away from meaning and fullness and still working hard to acquire the possessions you want. The doorway we speak of opens to a way of living in the world where noth-

*ing is "out there and far away" but instead "within you and very close."*

*The new life is the life of union with all things, beginning with yourself. It is a way of being in your own life and world and seeing it as lovingly held together and in union with all that is. It is as if you rest in the deep warmth of your bathtub with all of what you desire there in the tub with you. In the substance of this beautiful tub of water, everything is connected. There is no need for grasping or clutching anything for everything is here with you and for you. It cannot escape either! The main "work" is to rest and be nourished, allowing what is already present and complete to come to you.*

*You have had tastes of this life when everything seemed to fall in its place naturally and easily. Times of No Escape are doorways into a relationship with life, where this experience becomes a sustainable way of living in the world. Is this not why you chose to experience interim places? To teach about this new life? Yes, it is!*

## ☽ Tools for the Journey

### What to do when there is No Escape:

➤ When all paths of escape are blocked, assume it is time to stand still.

➤ Stop running, hiding, blaming others and making excuses.

➤ Stop the activity and busyness.

➤ Find moments in which to quietly breathe, open yourself now to receive a response from your sacred self (not your scared self), the one who has been with you from the beginning.

➤ Know that you are strong and courageous for ceasing much of your activity to turn and face yourself in this moment. Few people do this, choosing instead to stay busy. Your response draws a powerful response from the universe.

➤ Continue the active work of being compassionate and patient with yourself even though this action seems irrelevant.

➤ As always, surrender all concerns and doubts.

➤ Practice gratitude; build into your days quiet moments for offering thanks.

➤ Continue keeping notes of what happens when you surrender something to spirit.

➤ Remember, you are building credible evidence of a different, more powerful way of living.

## ☽ Summary

Interim places are the desolate regions your life calls you into after the old path you have followed disappears and before you know the new way. You feel lost without any direction or sense of what has happened to you or why. In this section, I have suggested that these times are not flukes, not mistakes, not punishment from the gods. Rather they are invitations to fully inhabit your life.

Interim places are rarely neon lit or glossy places, and they never show up on the covers of magazines in the business or vacation sections of the bookstore. Your life seems to call you back to the inner world you left long ago for another world. In returning, you must not lose the external world you have come to know so well. Instead, you deepen your connection with your original soulful world so that you might go back into the external world with a more grounded yet divinely powered perspective. Your relationship with your world has begun to change in a profound way.

You may not be finished with this time or terrain yet, but you are well on your way. There are still more spirit-freeing lessons to this interim place school!

# Constellation

*I looked into the night sky*
*and saw stars burning in bright constellations*
*that we give names to*
*and I believed that I too was a constellation—*
*made up of many bright and burning parts.*
*Then the night came down into my life,*
*an unknown destroyer loose in my home at night,*
*and opened me as I watched.*
*There was nothing else I could do.*

*All the constellations disappeared*
*and so did I.*
*Only then, my Life shined brighter*
*and more beautifully than all constellations*
*and beyond all names.*
*The night showed me this.*

— D.H.[1]

### CHAPTER 7

# The Great Exchange: Our Grief Cry for Transformation

Surrendering as an act of strength

I used to believe I was like a constellation of stars. I thought the sky mirrored how people were configured. The brightest stars in my constellation were stars of achievement, financial wealth and well-being, success, respect, and admiration from important others, fatherhood, husbandhood, and bodily health. One by one, all the stars burned out. Lost between lives is a story of losing what seems important only to find something much greater and more precious in its place. Later.

We have learned that interim places are about our growth and transformation, but what do we actually lose and what does the universe offer us in exchange? Exploring this "great exchange" we'll find we often experience a series of losses:

➤ Losing the imaginary self

➤ Losing the figurine God

➤ Losing a sense of place and then a subtle, but significant, growth:

➤ Shifting our stance toward fear

➤ Freeing the interior voice

# ❯ *Secret openings, hidden doorways: recognizing the signposts*

Despite what you see and feel in this terrain, you stand on the verge of a great exchange with the universe. The litmus test or markers designating breakthrough are not the kind you are accustomed to seeing. My experience suggests any of the following symptoms would be worth paying attention to, as they indicate the presence of new life trying to break through to you:

➤ You feel so stuck in the crumbling debris of your life that you can neither turn back nor move forward;

➤ You are on an exhausting treadmill of hard work, endless demands on your time and energy, expectations of sustained perfection or at least high achievement, and you experience mostly a nagging emptiness inside;

➤ You have lost a sense of satisfaction and meaning and you don't know where to find it. You have tried to do what the world says you should do. Perhaps you succeeded; perhaps you failed. Either way, it doesn't matter to you anymore;

➤ You feel yourself coming unglued inside; nobody else may know it, but you do. You feel weak, frightened, and very tired. You allow yourself little freedom to experience this and would never allow yourself to speak about it;

➤ You have trouble quieting your mind, yet you know at a deep level that this is exactly what you need to do.

We have talked about exchanging our grief (anger, fear, denial, etc.) for transformation earlier during our passage through the different terrains of interim places. As we move into and through No Escape, however, our questions have changed, as has our very relationship with our own life! Something much deeper is at stake than simply surviving a tough life transition, and again we'll examine the exchange we have been looking at from Rilke[2] :

*I'm such a long way in I can see no way through*
*and no space, everything is close to my face*
*and everything close to my face is stone.*
*I do not have much knowledge yet in grief*
*so this massive darkness makes me feel small.*
*You be the master, make yourself fierce and break in*
*then your great transforming will happen to me*
*and my great grief cry will happen to you.*

## ☽ *Real loss and imaginary loss*

Real loss has always had to do with the loss of solid things in the external world. People die. Property is lost, jobs disappear, lifestyles come and go. Health is compromised. Physical mobility is challenged. Everything is in constant motion. This is the nature of all living things. Imaginary loss has been relegated to the interior world, which our culture defines as a lesser world. Imaginary loss has to do with what we think, feel, and imagine; elements that are seen in our society as less important than what we can see and touch. However, in interim places everything turns inside out. The interior life crashes to the forefront, demanding we recognize two key realities: that what we have held as real— externalized definitions of self-worth and value—is largely

imaginary and that what we have dismissed as imaginary—
deep internal dialogue and knowing—is very real indeed.

You experience three essential losses in interim places
which leave you with a better understanding of what your
sacred self is after. Each of these losses is an interior loss,
part real and part imaginary. They continue to strike a significant blow to who you are and to how you make sense
out of your life. Interior shifts, like these, often coincide
with real events in your external life but sometimes the
inner disruption far exceeds the precipitating events. It is as
if your sacred self uses the circumstances of your life to
effect a far greater transformation than circumstances
would seem to warrant. Each loss feels very personal and
leaves you feeling fragile for a period of time because these
losses heal the tender place of the heart.

# ❯ *Losing the imaginary self*

Interim places break the image you have of yourself, and
the universe is a compassionate craftsman. It allows you to
experience the impossible demands of being trapped in the
small boxes you carve out for your very large, magnificent
self. It then sets a trap, which may be sprung either by success or by failure. You may achieve everything you
thought would give you meaning and satisfaction, only to
discover you still feel restless, bored, and far away from
anything that matters. Or, you may fail at something so
significant that you were convinced it would kill you, but
you find in the aftermath you are still very much alive. If
you are sincere in these moments, you realize and accept
that something inside you must shift to accommodate this
unexpected reality.

It can be terrifying and disorienting to lose everything
you thought made you who you are and *then to find your-*

*self still alive.* Imaginary self-loss has to do with the loss of images, assumptions, and stories you tell yourself about how you should be and about how your life should appear. Christopher Reeve and others who have suffered devastating and life-altering changes in their bodies can speak of these losses. Yes, you are alive. Yes, others are happy you are alive. But these losses cut deep into your being. So, no, you may not want to be here. You may feel dead or feel like you should be. And for you, those feelings are valid because a part of you *is* dying and needs to be allowed to die.

This inner loss of who we thought we were affects many of us, even though outwardly our lives and bodies may appear as they always have. The universe does not operate with bells and whistles but instead with understated efficiency. It seldom draws attention to the deeper work it effects in us. In the image-breaking moments we encounter in interim places, we are called by the sacred self to another, inner world. If we turn away, we may wander around empty for years. If we accept the challenge and turn inward, the answers we seek will appear. The truth we need will come to us, the wisdom we hunger for will find us. The "great grief cry," utterly devalued by our culture, is the doorway to a deeper partnership with the sacred which holds the transforming power, meaning, and solutions we seek. I now understand that standing in this space is the work of becoming a true spiritual warrior.

The bottom line is this: you turn inward because you know you need to. You cannot explain why you make this turn. Then something begins to shift, slowly, over the course of many months. You begin to see how fundamentally afraid you are of simply being with yourself, afraid of what you will see and feel. You begin to see how many of your actions and habits reinforce a sense of separation from yourself.

# ❯ Secret openings, hidden doorways: recognizing the signposts that indicate new life approaches!

**Do you find ways to avoid being with yourself? Do you:**

➤ Fill quiet time with noise?

➤ Fill reflection time with activity?

➤ Avoid time alone completely?

➤ Dismiss as unimportant things that simply bring you joy (i.e., going to a matinee, buying flowers, walking, playing?)

➤ Have tremendous trouble simply quieting your mind?

➤ Have a hard time giving yourself permission to relax and waste time well?

➤ Have trouble showing up and being present with your family or friends?

➤ Feel you must be "on" around others and give a good performance?

➤ Feel uncomfortable with confusion and uncertainty, and prefer to appear as though you know and understand everything?

➤ Rarely celebrate achievements because you believe you are only as good as your next one?

➤ Dismiss your giftedness as irrelevant and not worth feeling good about?

If you answered yes to any of these statements, you must turn inward. You must realize that who you really are far surpasses the image you strive to maintain. My ideal imaginary self was built around perfection and competence. I always needed to be perfect at everything I did. A true son of an alcoholic, where value is only assigned outwardly, in the world of doing and activity. Never inwardly, where intimacy, trust, and vulnerability are required to open up the life so its greatness can be manifested. Your sacred self, your essential self, has brought you to this moment. It has not been your personality, your mind, or some strange set of circumstances. This time has been carefully orchestrated for you. Pay attention to the subtle signposts above. Your next reminders will not be so subtle.

Your ideal and imaginary image is a powerful and devastating force. It is never really satisfied and never rests. This image is only interested in safety and comfort and pursues both by setting impossible standards of perfection and punishing all your efforts that fell short. And all of your efforts feel as though they fall short. That's the point of having an ideal and imaginary self.

You're invited to see the game your mind has been playing with you all along. You thought you would be safe and worthwhile if you played; instead, you have been killing yourself. The sweet flowing water you desired has become fire.

Achievement is fine, but the compulsive need to achieve is destructive. Continuous improvement is fine, but the compulsive need to strive, the relentless quest to punish anything short of perfection will take years off of your life and ruin every day. While you are in the grip of your imaginary self, you stop experiencing the real you and stop responding to the life you actually are given to live today. At home, you keep yourself hidden away from conflicts and even intimate dialogue because your ideal image convinces you that what is hidden in you needs to remain hidden. If others discovered who you really are, something very bad will happen. Vulnerability and authenticity are dangerous to the imaginary self.

At work and at home when legitimate feedback is given you, you reject it if you feel it reveals something about you that runs contrary to the image you have of who you are. Or you take it in and allow it to simmer and boil within you. Image is so insidious that you seldom question whether it is any different from who you really are. You begin to see, in interim places, that you have been responding to this false image of yourself for a long, long time. In my case, many years.

**Your sacred self has carefully
arranged the whole catastrophe!**

The imaginary self tells lies about who we really are and who we can really be. Because we believe them, the lies keep us in very small boxes. The lies always have a threat attached to them: Be this way or else . . . Keep your true viewpoints to yourself or else . . . Behave this way or some-thing bad will happen to you . . . Never let them see you sweat or else . . . Fall in line or else . . Behave this way as a manager or else. These threats are seldom voiced or literal but rather are perceived in our bodies and felt as fear and stress. A tightening of the chest, neck, stomach, or shoul-ders often accompanies these perceived threats. They carry the full weight of impossibly fixed and certain reality. Rilke[3] described these threats in his poem: *"everything is close to my face and everything close to my face is stone."*

The deeper secret is that all of this has been arranged by the sacred self. It is not your mother's fault or your father's doing. It wasn't time before for you to see this; now is the time for your unfolding. Interim places are often the sacred self's response to the small boxes you made for yourself. The soul's strategy can be deceptively simple: through choice or misfortune you have violated a vow that your ideal self image said would "kill" you. Your survival causes fundamental shifts in your views of who you thought you were and what is genuinely possible for you. You have outgrown the images you have been holding of yourself. They must go. They were illusions anyway.

You cry out a great grief cry because it is not easy to break a vow you believe has kept you alive. It feels like death. If your vow has been to hide your true feelings and keep quiet, the first time you speak up when it matters will fill you with terror. If perfection has been part of your image and you have vowed to be perfect in every way, you will be devastated when something goes wrong publicly that reveals your imperfection. If power, invincibility, and invulnerability have been part of your image, then a near-fatal blow to your life and body may be necessary to help you see the small, thick box you have made to conceal the rich, tender humanity you have denied. If winning the approval of others has been your way of sealing your safety, self-worth and identity, then when powerful people are angry with you, you will be convinced your life may as well be over.

The imaginary self is an illusion. This is why it must go. This is why the sacred self, here to watch over and care for us, is so instrumental and ferocious in interim places. The sacred self assists us in coming to full expression of who we really are and does not rest until this work is completed. If we are faithful, interim places reveal who we are and who we are coming to be. During this process of "becoming," however, there is a gap that feels precarious. If you no longer seek approval when you meet someone important, what exactly will you do? If you lay aside perfectionism or control, what exactly is your role in the project team meeting today? Who will you be now? These issues take time and faithfulness to sort out. Only as illusion fades will your true life begin to shine through.

You are much greater and far more beautiful than all the stars and constellations in the sky!

The great transforming Rilke refers to is the sacred unfolding of ourselves in all of our magnificence and beauty. It is the universe revealing to us who we are and acknowledging its approval and love for us as we are. In exchange for that little self in a small box, with its grip on materialism, advancement, and social approval, we receive from the universe the continually deepening revelation of who we actually are. The challenge is to stand faithfully, as Rilke did, when all we have to offer the universe is our grief, or our fear and regret. When all you have to offer is your inner turmoil, know with certainty, "It is enough."

You must loosen your grasp and allow what you fear or grieve to slip into the hand of your sacred partner standing beside you. Then a space opens where you do not know what will happen next and it doesn't matter anymore. You expect nothing except to be met as one partner holds and supports the other. In this space, this interim space, an ordinary human moment is transformed into a sacred one where anything is possible.

When all light is gone from the path you are on, and you feel desperate and frightened, this transforming may mean nothing. Transforming does not make financial straits immediately go away. If you have made mistakes, there will still be consequences you have to face. If you are sick, there is no guarantee you will immediately recover your good health. But I argue for remembering the mystery of God. In the secret place of the heart we utter a grief cry and it is heard in the near vastness of heaven. This cry, sometimes so painful as to be only groaning without words, reaches the secret place of God and we are changed. Something beautiful begins to happen within us and within our circumstances. Our character is strengthened, and our capacities to endure a wider range of experiences within and without is established. Everything shifts only when we do.

It may be months or years before you can see it. However, along the way, almost imperceptibly at times, you become more fully human, more whole, more known to yourself and your Creator. You begin to fully inhabit your own life. You quietly become more spiritually fierce, able to stand, withstand, and prevail. Able to create from a different place within a life worth living. This is who you really are!

# ❥ *Tools for the Journey*
**What to do when the imaginary self begins to crumble:**

➤ Know with certainty this time will have an end. Sometimes you can only stand back and watch your life do what it needs to do; this is one of those times.

➤ Summon the courage to step back, stand down from your life, and rest.

➤ Using whatever amount of faith you have, surrender all concerns to Spirit.

➤ Know, with certainty, you've been heard. Look for nothing, expect nothing other than you have made contact with the sacred. Remember, there is more to who you are than the forceful or cautious part; the true You which lies waiting is much stronger, more balanced, and capable of great things—none of which may be visible from your current vantage point.

➤ Practice acknowledging out loud and then laying aside the societal messages you were given which served you in the past and kept you safe and alive; they may not serve you now. Remember, these old maps should have a "use by____" date stamped on them but we seldom pay attention! They're outdated. Lay them aside.

➤ Avoid excesses in alcohol, drugs, sex and activity that seems to have no purpose other than keeping you distracted. Some days you need a distraction; the issue here is excess.

➤ Do something fun the old you would never ordinarily do.

## ❱ Losing the figurine god

We all have certain expectations of God. We may trust God to provide our daily provisions of food, shelter, and clothing, and many of us have stories of miraculous provision. We never fear deprivation of these essentials, and some of us never fear losing our jobs and sources of funding for these things. I depended upon God for my sense of purpose and belongingness. I trusted him for health and healing. I trusted that my prayers would be answered like they always had been and that, even when I did not understand why something happened, I would see God's hand at work in delivering me to a stable place once again. Interim places were marked by a perceived absence of response from God.

It is significant that in many native cultures people celebrate the passage from adolescence to adulthood with sacred rituals introducing the young person to the ways of the Spirit. The rite of passage often is done alone. A solo trek, time spent alone in the wilderness, or like Jesus, a time of self-chosen deprivation in the wilderness of Judea, all seem to show that entrance into new life and power is initially done alone. Interim places often serve to bring us across a threshold into a place where we shed our old ways and beliefs related to God and we are clothed with new ways, new beliefs, and new power. And we travel through these regions alone. Or so it seems.

> ## Secret openings, hidden doorways: recognizing the signposts that indicate your God is too small and needs to expand for both you and God to go forward in partnership

The indicators below signify God within you, your sacred self, is busy drawing your attention to the need to let go of old, self-limiting definitions of God and of your too-small relationship with this God.

> ➤ You feel so afraid and alone and so abandoned by God.

> ➤ Familiar sources of support and resources disappear. Close colleagues go. Friends go. Home can go. Children can go. Brothers and sisters go. Familiar neighborhoods can go. Even heaven feels gone. You struggle to find replacements.

> ➤ Familiar ways of thinking and feeling about God and yourself that had always seemed right in the past are violated, or just no longer made sense to you. A good person

and close friend dies. A bad person, or someone you despise, comes into sudden wealth, success or happiness. You feel bewildered and betrayed. This discipline of dismay marks the path of any true spiritual seeker.

➤  Prayers appear to go unanswered.

➤   In your moments of desperation, you sometimes feel you have to beg God for just a scrap of blessing. Angered by this, you have a Scarlet O'Hara moment and vow to never live like this again. Strangely, this vow does elicit a response from the sacred: 'Great, now we can talk!'

➤  This response confuses and liberates you.

**Nothing is ever wasted by the sacred, although much is held until the right time**

Somewhere in heaven I am sure there is a clay vessel holding all the tears I cried when I made desperate prayers for deliverance. These prayers seemed to bring only silent indifference back from heaven. An entry from my journal reveals my desperate feelings at the time:

"Once, long ago, I had such strong faith. I could pray for anything and it would come to pass at some point before my eyes. Now only indifference and silence from You. You speak of friendship but Your silence would absolutely kill any human relationship. I look to the north and to the south hoping to find You there and, finding no one, turn to the east and west. Nothing. Only the wind and the moon in the night sky.

Will I ever feel Your arms around me again and the sweet presence of Your loving compassion and tenderness toward me? Will I ever know again Your assurance when all feels lost? Will I ever feel that I belong in this world with You beside me or will I go on as I am right now, feeling like an unwanted stranger and an intruder here? Will I ever again feel safe here or will this fear continue to choke me and rob me of the joy I once knew with You?

In these days of solitude I grip my life more tightly than ever before and I am more afraid than I ever was before. And so alone. Where are You when I cry? Do You hear me anymore? Is there no other way to advance in my life than by this solitary route? If this is the path to You then I reluctantly go on. Do I have a choice? I am too far in to turn around now."

Your brand of desperation may sound different, but if you have arrived at this point in the path, you have begun to change. You slowly become aware that you have never been alone and that your prayers and tears have been heard. (If you don't feel this way then act as if you do! Fake it 'til you make it. There are few things worse than feeling alone when you are not.) The sacred response, though, comes in very different ways than it has in the past. Interim places can be lonely proving grounds where the perception of God you go in with is not the same when you come out. You change. Because you change, your perception of God changes.

Something is burned out of you in interim places and something else is being burned into you. A sacred branding. You belong to yourself and your self in a new way. The great Sufi mystic, Rumi 4, had this to say in the thirteenth-century poem called, "Say Yes Quickly."

*Forget your life.*
*Say God is Great.*
*Get up.*
*You think you know what time it is.*
*It's time to pray.*
*You've carved so many little figurines, too many*
*. . . Tomorrow you'll see*

*what you've broken and torn tonight,*
*thrashing in the dark.*
*Inside you there's an artist you don't know about.*
*He's not interested in how things look different in*
*moonlight.*
*If you are here unfaithfully with us,*
*you're causing terrible damage.*
*If you've opened your loving to God's love,*
*you're helping people you don't know*
*and have never seen.*
*Is what I say true? Say yes quickly, . . .*

I entered interim places having carved so many little figurines out of a very dynamic God who refused to be boxed and tamed by me. My figurines included a God who would always honor my secret hope for safety, for quick fixes and instant deliverance. I wanted a god who would save me from myself and from pain and discomfort in my life. I wanted a God who would save me on my time schedule and would only work in ways that made sense to me; ways I could quickly see and understand. I had defined a god who would never confuse me or lead me into dismay. I feel foolish writing these statements, but I know each of us has our own irrational demands we make of God.

Something marvelous begins to happen, however, when the figurine gods we created refuse to show up. *We* begin to change. The partnership we have with the sacred can then become more authentic, more integral and vital. We begin to show up as equal, but very different partners.

Interim places reveal the mystery and wonder of God. These times bring you to a critical threshold in your life which, if successfully navigated, can transform the rest of your days. As you cross this threshold you realize, once again and more deeply than ever, that you are not designed to move through your life apart from the Divine. You are not expected to do this alone. Seeking the true partnership with your sacred self does not mean you are weak and feeble. Rather it means you have begun to wake up to who and what you are—a spiritual being—and that you have arrived at this juncture in the path of your life to claim your inheritance: partnership with your sacred essence.

As you dismantle your figurine gods and the false beliefs which support them, you begin to experience your own true spiritual capacity. You see and appreciate that you have grown weary in the past only when you felt you must somehow shoulder the full load of your life on your own. Even though we are not designed to do this, most of us persist in doing it anyway. There is simply too much that happens over which we have little or no control, so trying to move forward with any control-based strategy will fail. This weariness with a world that you rightly feel is sometimes overwhelming, coupled with a corresponding reluctance to turn and face yourself in quietness and faith, has brought you to the doorway of a new partnership with the sacred. You know you cannot go on as before. And you will not. There is no need to because something else has happened in you that surprises and alarms you.

You actively cultivate an on-going discipline of talking with your sacred partner, about more and more of what's really taking place in your life — the hard reality you're up against, the difficulty of surrendering those things over which you have little or no control, the frustration and anger at feeling so confused and helpless at times. A friendship develops between the two of you. For the first time you get the sense this partnership has two equal, but different, parties — you and your sacred self. The two of you are joined by a shared purpose: to open the fullness of your life.

# ❯ The difference between dependency and interdependency

I come from a Judeo-Christian background and have a strong and vital relationship with the person of Jesus Christ. This feels awkward to write about because the words have so much baggage for some. One of the cool aspects of how Jesus ministered is His frequent use of *dismay* as a teaching tool. When I read scripture, Jesus seems to frequently upset His true disciples by who He hangs out with, what He says to those in authority, and by what He does or refuses to do. He always expands the boxes of understanding. He never seems to me to foster a dependency upon Himself and instead talks of friendship (i.e., interdependency) with God as a real option.

I have struggled over the years with a sense of dependency upon God that felt out of balance. I was clear on what I needed from God but seldom felt clear on what God needed from me. The idea of continual repentance from sin seemed like a marketing ploy, and one that has a built-in dependency with it. This never sat right with me. It now seems to me that God desires that I fully inhabit the life I'm living and to do so with the full resourcefulness of heaven within and without. The sacred self seems to be that aspect of me that is most directly connected to the sacred and, as a point and place of contact within my body, feels like a core part of my interdependency with God. An individual pillar of fire within me that both receives (needed supply) from heaven and offers (my grief cry and gratefulness) in exchange.

The sacred self ushers in a refreshing appreciation for your own complexity and magnificence for which there is room to feel very grateful. As my level of openness expands, I am open to experiencing a wonderfully alive relationship with the Jesus I personally know, which, I am quick to say, is not to be confused with the magazine and televangelized versions.

I say all of this to make this point: contact with the sacred self expands and deepens the relationship you have with God, as you understand God.

## ❯ *Tools for the Journey*

**What to do when the figurine god disappears:**

➤ Do not trust and act upon only what you see and hear physically; find ways to quiet yourself by walking, running, or sitting so you can hear your body's wisdom or knowing.

➤ Stop analyzing and evaluating the deeper current of your life. It runs on a different time, pace, and schedule. It is always right even though you may feel it is too late or premature. Step into and experience each day without understanding or knowing why.

➤ Remember that every day, every experience, is sacred, especially the moment after surrender. You may feel like nothing is happening in your life and that you're going nowhere, but nothing is wasted by the universe. Old parts of you are dying now; you're likely to feel down, confused, bored or lost. Accept that feeling this way is okay and then choose to do something you enjoy.

➤ Surrender. Each day, many times a day if needed, allow the weight of worry to slip from your shoulders.

➤ Get quiet. Breathe deeply. Relax into the present moment. You can be clear about results you desire without knowing how or where to begin. Find what your real intention is now (receiving) and entrust into the hands of the sacred what you cannot control (giving).

# 〉 *Losing a sense of place*

Losing touch with where you are in life, losing a sense of place, can be terrifying. The maps you use to mark your "locations" typically have only external reference points: employment, financial wealth, steady and increasing income levels, home, mortgage, investment portfolios, health for your loved ones and plans for the future. When any one of these markers disappears, you feel fear or uncertainty. When many of them disappear, as they can during interim places, there can be an extended period of time when you really don't know where you are anymore.

You never know how much you referenced the external world and its signposts to help you know where you are in your life until your world goes dark with loss. For many years you belonged to the world more than you belonged to yourself. You belonged to your work, to your employer, to others' approval and respect of you and to their notions of success and advancement. You gave yourself over, at times, to others' definitions of what it meant to be a real man or woman and a worthwhile person, a good parent and a spiritual person.

Some of these areas are good and worthy, but you and I give ourselves away in the wrong way. When large parcels of our lives are given over to external things (others' opinions and reinforcement), we no longer belong to ourselves. We belong to that to which we have attached ourselves. It is dangerous to belong to the world more than you belong to yourself. We have already seen that when there are whole regions in us that we are afraid to look at, acknowledge or draw near to, these parts belong to our fear, not to us. Your sacred self wants you to come home to your expanded self, to your own unique and precious life.

In order to belong to your own life you must be able to come home and rest with all of who you are. This takes time and occurs bit by bit. You show up in parts. Little by little, you bring more of yourself into the loving consciousness with which you are created and from which you strayed. It sometimes takes the loss of many external attachments to teach us the beginning way to belong to ourselves and to the spiritual capacity within. As you open to more of your experience you find it easier (though still a struggle at times) to rest in the flow of your life and simply trust your expanded capacity to respond. This is the great transforming Rilke talked about.

As an added benefit, you discover that as you belong to more and more of your own interior regions (your joys, griefs, fears, and loneliness), you are more able to be at home with others. A more diverse group of others. You no longer hide as much. You slowly begin to have more authentic conversations and relationships and to feel more alive and whole in them.

## ❯ Secret openings, hidden doorways: recognizing the guideposts calling for new maps to locate where you are and where you need to be

The following are actually signs of health even though when you come to experience them you tell yourself that they are signs that you are becoming unglued:

➤ You reluctantly acknowledge that the days you have are not, on average, the days you want to be in.

➤ You have a gut instinct that change is needed and, even though you may not know what or how this will happen, you know you must not ignore your intuition.

➤ Your body has begun to give you wake up calls saying that you simply cannot continue living as you are. Sickness, injury, small or large accidents, sleeplessness, depression are possible symptoms. These symptoms appear to be escalating and you feel alarmed.

➤ You've become what the culture says you should become and have acquired what you "should" acquire, yet you feel ambivalent or bored with your life.

➤ Conversely, you have lost or stepped away from the culturally prescribed life and suddenly feel "alive" again.

➤ You find yourself daydreaming, praying, meditating, seeking, or just longing for some deeper connection or sense of belongingness that you have as yet no language for. It feels essential.

➤ You have lost your sense of vision or purpose and wander around as if cast adrift without an anchor. The open space seems both refreshing and scary.

### Are you really lost or just looking at external reference points?

I continue to find it difficult to describe a sense of place without referencing external standards. The truth is that when I reference internal standards I feel I can give a precise description of where I am. It's just that my externally referenced self shakes its head in disapproval. It is possible to be very clear, internally, of where you are even when the external circumstances are confusing. Here's how my dialogue sounds:

## ❭ *Voice of the internal self*

"I am more than fifty years old and feel more alive, more vital, than ever before. I have boundless energy, an abiding sense of curiosity and mischief that I haven't experienced since boyhood, and an excitement about today and tomorrow. I could die today and honestly say, 'It's a good day to die', because I have lived fully. I love and open myself to love. I know how to be intimate and sensual and have finally linked these with sexuality after trying hard for many years. Suddenly, making love is possible instead of having sex, and these are the most joyful moments of my life. I have known creative success in my work and have seen the impact my presence and contribution has on others. I know it is good.

"I have a deep sense of the sacred presence every day. I feel joy in the small and big things of beauty each day. I cry in all the right places at movies and am also moved to tears by thunderstorms and snowfall. I can work and earn money or I can not work. I no longer need to work in order to feel good about who I am. When I do work, therefore, I am doing the best work of my life because I show up with fewer and fewer strings attached to the outcomes. I fully invest myself in all I do, but walk away from it all at the end of the day and sleep deeply during the night.

"I love my partner, Lisa, and want to continue growing alongside her. I count it a deep honor simply to be in her presence. I have quality time with my daughter, Cate, that most fathers never knew they needed, let alone set time aside to pursue. When I work with esteemed colleagues around whom I once felt intimidated, I now know them as partners with me. I enjoy their brilliance and giftedness without diminishing my own. To me, this feels like a huge shift, though I do not know or remember when it happened or if I was there when it did.

"I still have concerns about my future. I wrestle with doubt and depression at times. I have a sense these interim places will turn out okay, but I do not know for sure any-more than anyone else does. I am alive today. I feel grateful. I am not just a visitor in my life anymore but I inhabit more and more of my life. Nothing really important happens much anymore. A walk by the ocean feels as important as a conference I facilitate with CEOs. Playing with my daugh-ter or with my loving partner seems to be the best way to prepare for a demanding week of work. I feel very alive even when I am in despair, concerned over how little I have to show for my life up to this point.

"I realize in these moments of not knowing that I actu-ally know much about where I am. It's just that I am using different maps and reference points."

## ❱ *Voice of the external self*

"I am more than fifty years old. I should be financially well off like I once was. Now I am not sure how I will pay my taxes let alone meet next month's obligations. I should be doing great and important things with my life. I should be in great demand as a speaker and facilitator. I have such great things to say—I am afraid the world will never completely discover me. I fear dying as an old man and looking back with regret at how little I did with my life. I should be bigger than I am by now. The two years that have already been lost in interim places are irreplaceable; I will never catch up and make up for the time and money I lost wandering around in the dark.

"Happiness is irrelevant. Nice if you have it, but it counts for nothing in the bigger picture of things. Maybe God doesn't use me because I really have little to offer. I am slipping further and further behind and need to grab hold of my life and get busy. I need to do something. All the time I spend moving with the life I have is wasted—I could be forcing bigger and more important circles to open up.

"Love and surrender, awareness and intimacy do not matter at all. I need to do something important. I need to do something more tomorrow. I must keep moving. I cannot trust God to help me with my future, he has done all He could. If I don't take it all upon my shoulders, it will not get done. Anything surrendered is lost forever. Try harder, work harder. I must do something important or I will grow old and die wishing I had."

The poet Rilke[5] once described living with the tension of these two opposing voices within:

> *I am the rest between two notes*
> *that are somehow always in discord*
> *because death's note wants to climb over.*
> *But in the dark interval,*
> *reconciled,*
> *they stand there trembling.*
> *And the song goes on beautiful.*

We need both perspectives to fully inhabit our lives, to be fully human. As we create an accurate sense of place, we have two voices within that vie for our attention. The external voice, named because of its strong cultural message to us as men and women, has something to offer that we want to pay attention to. If we lose contact with this voice, we lose contact with the world, the world in which we contribute our gifts. If we live only according to this externally referenced place, however, it will kill us with its relentless comparisons, its suffocating fears, jealousies, and revenge, and its thick, impenetrable illusion of what is real. We need our true voice, our internal voice, to help us remember who we are and to shape and anchor our contribution to the world.

For a very long time, you may seldom have recognized your internal voice and did not trust it when you heard it. Now think of it as the voice of your sacred self. It values life and living above everything else, including much of what your external voice sets up as standards for a valuable life. The internal voice sees reality as opaque; even harsh reality is open to many interpretations and may lead anywhere. The external sees reality as fixed and given. There is always a logical reason to fear. The external antidote to fear is always to be more and to do more and to defend against others who want what you have. The internal is open to doing and being more, too, but often wants to wait, inquire, and move with the deeper forces of life that may be in play. Interim places show the limitations of living only to the demands of the external voice of the world and open the door to living as *the rest between two notes* that are somehow always in discord.

## ☽ *Tools for the Journey*

**When we've lost our sense of place.**
**What to do when our external signposts disappear:**

➤ Avoid excesses in alcohol, drugs, sex, work, inane activity, and other addictions. This is a significant time of realignment down to the cellular level. Be present for it!

➤ Feel the weight and value you have assigned to the societal standards from which you are breaking free. For most of us they are based upon fear; below the fear you will find anger, and below the anger, sadness. Get in touch with the sadness—what does it say to you? Hint: somewhere along the line, you stopped playing your own unique tune.

➤ Ask yourself if these external standards define your true essence, the "all of me" that defies any box you might put around it. Do not give yourself away to standards which exist outside of yourself. They are too small for you!

➤ Cultivate silence, attentiveness, and relationships to key people in your life. Find a balance between healthy solitude and unhealthy isolation.

➤ Get in touch with nature, which continues on its intended way regardless of small crises we experience. The "nature" of nature shows us how we should relate to interim places: this period of your life, too, will pass. Go on your way and experience everything, but hold onto nothing.

➤ Recognize that old definitions of yourself are passing away and that you are grieving the loss. Grief seldom shows up in a nicely wrapped package that says, "Grief, please handle with care." You may instead feel ugly, worthless, and quite useless. Give your grief to the sacred and you will receive a new and greater life back. Trust me on this.

## ❯ *Shifting your stance toward fear*

Interim places are a pathway into fear. Yet when you live with fearful circumstances you once thought would kill you and discover they don't, your relationship with fear itself changes. Your relationship with your own capacity changes. You have by now realized that you feared your own capacity. You have secretly thought, "Surely when this catastrophe happens I won't be able to handle it and I will perish." You have not died yet. As you continue to break free from this narrow, fearful view of your capacity, you notice that God breaks out of the porcelain mold you have held Him in and He becomes more real too. Walking through the things that bring you fear enables you to see the transforming power of the invisible. But you have to walk through. This is how you are enlarged.

Fear holds a gift you receive in no other way or place. Rilke knew this. That's why he stood still. That's why you quiet yourself and stand still too. In this quiet place you hear what you need to hear and know what you need to do when you need to know it. Not before. You continue to discover, day by day, the simplicity of resting in the present moment and trusting the sacred capacity within.

## ❯ A revised definition of what it means to be a strong spiritual warrior

Several times I have seen, in vision form during a daydream or while on a jog, what it means to be spiritually strong. It means being able to see and move with the subtle, nimble moves of Spirit. To follow the lead of the universe, to stand still when it does, to move gently when it does, to move in aggressively when it does. But always moving in concert with Spirit, never lagging behind or racing ahead. It takes a lifetime of faith, skill, and discipline to learn this art. I have valued only the action part of strength; now I am beginning to see the power of harmony, quietness, and attentive strength as well. To be spiritually strong means moving with Spirit and speaking with my true voice, the voice that lies waiting on the other side of fear.

# ❯ *Surrendering as an act of strength*

To most people surrendering means giving up. It means to resign, to turn away from or to quit. In the journey of finding your essential voice, surrender takes on a very different meaning: to invoke, invite in, elicit assistance from, release with love, to draw forth new energy. In your story of moving through the fear and uncertainty of interim places, you learn to surrender as an act of strength. You uncover the truth that when you are at the end of the power of your personality, this is the beginning of your real power—the power that proceeds forth from the sacred partner within.

Rumi[6] says, *"Inside you there's an artist you don't know about. He's not interested in how things look different in moonlight."* Although you do not always sense the presence of this artist within, you have a deep knowing that this artist is your true essence, that core aspect of you infused with the Spirit of God. It is this sacred self that draws you into the land of loss and grief. Your sacred self knows there are old ways in you that must be exposed to the light and truth so they will lose their illusory grip on you. You know that to be here unfaithfully means to choose to continue living in illusion and you don't want to live and work like this any further. You've lost your taste for the sweet water of comfort and have developed instead a taste for fire. Resolve: "If I am to go down I'll damn well go down in flames!"

Surrender is critical because the struggle we carry within and around us is, at times, overwhelming and demanding. The small boxes we have carved out for our lives have no way out: we need someone to break in. Surrender is an active invitation for the spirit dimension to come forth, intervene in our circumstances and henceforth walk with us. Again, Rilke's[7] stance reveals the simplicity of this action:

*You be the master,*
*make yourself fierce and break in,*
*then your great transforming will happen to me*
*and my great grief cry will happen to you.*

There are no strings attached with the poet's surrender, no demands that the response be quick, cost effective, pleasing to those who we live and work with, measurable or even understandable to us. There is no proviso stipulating how spirit can move or whose permission must first be received before action is undertaken. Surrender means you release your grief and all concerns that surround it to spirit. You open yourself to receiving back transformation. No strings attached.

You've been trained in the landscape of No Light, All is Lost, No End in Sight and finally, No Escape. You have been disciplined to quiet yourself and to acknowledge that, at times like these, the best you can do is stand still and acknowledge there are forces in play that are beyond your meager abilities to control. You release your well-constructed plans and endless expectations for the transforming life of spirit.

No bartering, no demands.

The simplicity of this exchange is the kind of simplicity that costs everything!

# ❱ *The Sacred Self observes*

*To open the heart is to open yourself to being fully human. Many people incorrectly assume that what distinguishes humans from other species is intellect. While this has an obvious element of truth to it on the earth, your intellect is not what distinguishes you elsewhere in the universe. There are countless beings and civilizations with greater intellectual capacities than humans; nevertheless, the entire created universe knows of your human race. They know you because of your heart.*

*You, dearest one, have chosen to come again to this earth to open your heart further. Others who read these words have done the same. Each life is different and the specific heart issues to be addressed are different. Some come to heal from betrayal and loss while others work out issues of control, abandonment and surrender. Still others address union with essence and new levels of interdependence and co-creation with the universe. These are all matters of the open heart. Do you see?*

*The small ego mind does not care for this at all and sets forth all manner of illusion to maintain its own appearance of control. It does so with the full blessing of Spirit. It has not been time for people with full and open hearts to walk your earth. In the past, many were killed who spoke truth from the heart and many others were ostracized, ridiculed and condemned by their families, communities, and established systems of education, religion, and business (including the media). It has not been time until now. Now is the time for the people like you, dearest brother in the light, to come forward with what you know about love, about true power that heals and does not destroy, and about living and working in abundant union with Spirit, with your sacred self and with others.*

*It is the open heart that knows of these things because the open heart is oriented toward and recognizes truth. For many, the first move towards truth feels threatening because the heart recognizes illusion that must go.*

*Illusion masquerades as truth, feels like truth, is talked about and held as truth, but cannot liberate the heart as only truth can. Illusion constricts the heart (literally), weakens the body's immune system, drains vitality from the individual, and erodes community and generative creativity with others. The work of walking through illusion, seeing it and feeling its weight is not easy. It feels like you are dismantling your own life with little to show for the pain you feel and no way of knowing whether you are moving toward something greater or dying where you stand. It often feels like a solitary journey, one that is kept hidden from others because your culture places no value on this inward attention.*

*We wish to say two things to you. First, you are never alone or separated from divine love. You are more precious than it is possible now for you to understand, but if you are quiet you can know this truth in your heart. You are never separated from the presence of love. Second, the work of seeing through illusion to truth is a sacred capacity of yours and there is much support for you in this process. You may see or feel nothing; you may wonder if your life matters to anyone or has any meaning at all. We encourage you to give these thoughts and wonderings room to simply be in you and move through you. It simply means that an old part of you is dying now and will be replaced by new and greater life.*

*You are not lost. You are simply in a place called "Lost," and these are common feelings associated with this place. Do what the great poet did: stand and surrender all to Spirit . . . "Let my great grief cry happen to you and your great transforming happen to me . . ."*

*And continue your journey.*

# Reminders

*Before dawn, across the whole road*
*as I pass I feel spiderwebs.*
*Within people's voices, under their words or*
*woven into the pauses, I hear a hidden sound.*
*One thin green light flashes over a smooth sea*
*just as the sun goes down.*
*What roses lie on the altar of evening*
*I inhale carefully, to keep more of.*
*Tasting all these and letting them have*
*their ways to waken me, I shiver and resolve:*
*In my life, I will more than live.*

— William Stafford[1]

### CHAPTER 8

# Knowing with an Open Heart

The deeper walk of surrender: reclaiming the first life

THERE is one thing upon which all religions and spiritual traditions agree. It is that to become fully human and *more than live* requires that we open our heart to life. In the previous chapters we have talked about surrender and how the loss of illusion helps us to see ourselves more clearly. As we surrender what we cannot control and open our heart to experiencing the life that is happening within and around us right now, we become changed.

The heart wants to open to the fullness of experience and to the beauty and struggle that are found in our life today. It is in this opening that we find the fullness of God within, our true essence and the seeds of a new way to live and contribute in the world.

Sadly, you may not have even considered your heart was worth knowing at all let alone opening to it and trusting it. I came to the task of knowing the heart late in the game but not too late for me to know the joy and peace and excitement that only the open heart can bring. Your own attempt to live a rational, organized and planful life has shown you, in interim places, that life does not work this way. The intellect alone, no matter how formidable, cannot grapple with the complexity of life on its own. Your head only knows how to do what has been done before, with small incremental adjustments it defines as progress. The stance of analyzing and evaluating life is simply not up to the challenge of responding to the complexity of life today.

## ❯ Secret openings, hidden doorways: recognizing when your heart needs to open

➤ You have increasing difficulty holding a thought in your head that does not have you at the center of it; the thoughts you hold tend towards anxiety.

➤ You find yourself comparing yourself to others in ways that leave you feeling "less than."

➤ You notice yourself becoming more judgmental and harsh across a wider set of circumstances and people.

➤ You worry about not measuring up.

➤ You have trouble resting, enjoying free time, and simply laying low.

➤ A physical tightening of the chest, neck and shoulders marks most of your days.

➤ You cannot remember the last time you had fun.

The most important issues of your life are not issues of the head at all but rather matters of the heart. Relationships, family, contributing to community, finding ways to authentically influence and impact others, and summoning the courage to speak your own voice in the world are first and foremost matters of the heart. It takes an engaged and opened heart to sort through them and even then, it is hard.

I want to speak of several related matters of the heart in this chapter, areas where openness is needed so light and clarity may enter. Each of these issues is a challenge or paradox to the intellect. The mind sees them as impossible dilemmas which have troubled me greatly during interim places. Yet, an opened heart sees them as threshold opportunities to expand our capacity to live with gratitude and compassion towards self and others. The opened heart offers them as direction.

## ) Let go of attachments to the past and future

If we had no memory we would not suffer at all. Suffering is the emotional baggage left over from old wounds and from comparisons to old images of what we should be and how far along we should have come by now. Comparisons with old expectations are the jagged edge we slide along during interim places. When the path ahead is lost the old voices cry out, "You fool." And, weakened by 'not knowing' in a culture where we are always supposed to know where we are, we make ourselves vulnerable to their torments.

The main issue in opening your heart is control: where do you choose to abide each day? Do you choose a relationship with your essential, sacred center today, in this moment or with your imaginary self and its concerns about yesterday and tomorrow? Each day you make this choice. The imaginary self says you will lose your edge if you stop thinking about the future, or you will lose respect if you let go of what may have been yours in the past. Both statements are lies that will keep you from the life you've come here to live today.

The imaginary self lives only in the past and future. You already know about your imaginary self; this aspect of you knows that if it sets the comparison bar high enough you will only fail. Your failure results in your clinging even tighter to the delusion the imaginary self spins, as if to confirm it. So, the bar is set at idealized and unreachable heights. These standards are sunk deep into the ground of your psyche through pillars of comparison to the past and future that leave you feeling always less than others. "I could have . . . I should have . . . I have to . . . I'll be happy when . . . If only . . ." are its siren cries.

The songs are different for each person yet strangely always the same: "You're too slow . . . You cannot write . . . You're too quiet . . . You cannot possibly be in a relationship that endures . . . You're not cut out for your work . . . You should be like . . ." You come to dread the presence of this side of yourself because the comparisons all seem so true. They strike the soft, vulnerable and wounded place within, the core delusion you have always carried around your neck. Your heart wants you to become intimately familiar with this place now not so you can then compensate but so you can open to the truth beneath the illusion.

## ❯ The great and hidden secret we each carry

This soft place, darkened like a cave with no exit or entrance, conceals a core, false belief that simply says:

> *I am not lovable or worthy of love as I am.*
> *I need to do or be something other than who*
> *I am in order to matter.*

Any comparison you choose to believe, you do so only because it confirms, however secretly and unconsciously, this core place of delusion in yourself. If it did not strike so close to this vulnerable center you would dismiss it as foolishness immediately.

This is the compensatory underside of vision. If the new hospital wing that has gone empty in town since it went up four years ago could speak, it would tell a story about how it was a mere monument to the fragile underside of the CEO who was also looking to make his life important and real. The action we take from such a place within, even when it appears strong, is just compensatory. A reaction to the fear we feel when we believe we're not worthy or worth loving as we are.

## ❯ *Recognizing the call of your opening heart*

➤ Your ego only knows bigger, grander, glossier and more important. If you secretly feel small, irrelevant and not valuable or worthy, at times, big action and endless activity are a tempting snare. Instead of compensating, see the underlying delusion for the lie that it is. You're enough as you are!

➤ Look for small and large ways you try to make yourself bigger, more important and /or worry that you are none of these things.

➤ Delusion feels like a small, restricted, ugly, and fearful place within. Very secret, possibly even from you. Your life apparently thinks it is time for you to see and move past this dynamic into something greater. Acknowledge and surrender. You know the drill.

An open heart reveals the core place of delusion as well as the freedom it conceals. Most of us defend against ever seeing it by staying very busy and cluttering our lives with endless activities, work and any assortment of numbing strategies. Intimacy, in particular, is to be avoided. It is in the still moments of unbidden silence, however, that these old voices sing their harsh song. Maybe this is why these voices cry as loud as they now do: the sacred self wants us free.

The delusion in which you link your worth to anything external is a wound you no longer want to carry. It is *your oldest wound* the open heart seeks and reveals to us in interim places. Rilke[2] sums up the challenge of seeing things clearly:

> *What we fight against is so tiny,*
> *what fights with us is so great . . .*
> *if only we would let ourselves be dominated,*
> *as things do, by some immense storm,*
> *we would become strong too and not need*
> *names . . .*
> *When we win it's with small things and the*
> *triumph itself makes us small.*
> *What is extraordinary and eternal does not*
> *want to be bent by us.*

You slowly get clear in interim places that your life has been spent fighting many small fights that amount to nothing. As you regain your strength and courage you begin to draw closer to what is extraordinary within you. Standing between you and the vision and sense of purpose you want again to embody is the old delusion that you are innately not worthy as you are. It seldom announces itself so clearly and it is very elusive.

The core delusion you carry keeps you from living the

life you came here to live. It serves you a surrogate life instead. You may fight many small battles, at work and at home, grow to be very competent and win many of them; yet you will only feel exhausted and small at the end of the day. Some of us spend entire careers fighting small battles that, to our heart, are not worth fighting at all. What exactly are we trying to prove and to whom? The battles become our responsibilities, our days, our jobs, and our years. We grow weary and lose the vitality that was once ours.

### There is no "next bullet" to dodge, nothing you need to prove to anyone

The core delusion you carry tempts you to believe that if you do not continue to dodge the next bullet something bad will happen to you in the future. If you don't keep your truth to yourself others will find out what you really think and then you'll be in danger. If you don't keep tight control over others and what they do, they may do what they want without your managerial permission and then the whole show will come tumbling down. If you become vulnerable and feel your feelings, you will lose all control and never recover. If others see you being vulnerable it will mean they see you as weak and incapable of handling responsibility; your future career will be in ruins. Slowly, you see that to battle these fears is complete and utter foolishness.

Each small victory only adds to the power you assign the delusion already. Surrendering the small battles to spirit allows you opportunity to step back and ask whether the days you are in are the days your heart wants you to be in. The open heart knows what fear conceals. Fear is like the mother black bird in the fields I walked on as a boy. She feigns a broken wing when we approach, thinking she will play to our curiosity and draw us away from her nest. Fear takes us away from looking for the prize that often lies just behind it. Past the distractions that comparisons and compulsive behaviors offer us is the magnificent beauty the open heart wants to reveal about ourselves.

Seeing the delusion brings a felt shift within. Your whole body feels relieved. This realization of your innate worthiness and beauty is the golden elixir of which the mystics speak. It is freedom.

## ❯ The opened heart tells a different story as you listen and hear

➤ You already are enough as you are, nothing needs to be added.

➤ You are more than any definition, or any problem, or any struggle you happen to be having in any moment; no one issue defines you because, in essence, you are more than all definitions.

➤ You live in today. What you need for tomorrow will come to you when you need it. What is yours always comes to you. You cannot lose or miss what is yours.

➤ You have not been annihilated when you turned inward to face your fear; you are given life. You are able to handle anything your life presents you. You have extraordinary capacity.

➤ You are a complex and magnificent person.

You have been learning how to love and be present to yourself and others. These new capacities matter and impact all of your life and work. These qualities grow stronger now and are self contained: no comparisons with others or with some future state are necessary, thank you.

## No need to hide, you've been trained in the open landscape of interim places

There are no places to hide in interim places. There are no new jobs, new bosses or clients, no secret source of supply that can save you. Your own open heart finds you out. You are forced to be alone with yourself and with the illusions you have mistaken for you. Rilke says that which we most need to face in order to be made whole rolls over us like a storm across the fields. Our work is to surrender to it, to *allow ourselves be dominated, as things do, by some immense storm.*[3] The truth your heart carries, the storm, is your authentic, more than alive, essential self!

Here's an example of how insidious and clever our delusion can be and how immediately freeing it is to recognize it. Several years ago I struggled to learn the teaching design for a workshop I wanted to facilitate. Each outing felt awful and forced; I kept trying harder and harder to get it right but only became more stuck. Finally, after one especially difficult afternoon session, I went to dinner with my two co-facilitators. Barbara and Bob asked me how I was feeling because I had seemed very tense and stiff earlier. I told them how stuck I felt and then sighed, "I just want to master the content." The emphasis on mastery this early in the game was an indicator of my imaginary self and its impossible standards that, while laudable, were choking me. Barbara looked at me directly and said simply: "To hell with mastery. Talk about what you know."

Shortest coaching session I have ever had.

I recognized immediately that I had been trying to earn my way to self respect by trying hard to do great work instead of simply allowing my truth to be expressed. I was trying to not fail because to fail would confirm my belief that I was not enough. I felt a shift within as the core delusion was again touched and revealed. I went out the next day and had a wonderful day speaking my truth and touching others like I know I am able to.

Our heart depends on us to move through fear. This is the one movement we struggle so hard to make. It is only the unbidden silence and disruption of interim places that forces us into this deeper reflection. Surrendering the comparisons to yesterday and to what we should be tomorrow brings a new freedom to simply live and be alive today.

## ☽ *Turn and face now*

Most of my life has been spent living someplace other than here and now. If I look only at where my thoughts, concerns, feelings and desires have been directed, it is clear that they were directed to other times and places. When I look at my intimate relationships, which I have struggled with, it is true that while my body was present I was actually missing for large amounts of time during which the relationships were rumored to have taken place. I was someplace else, hidden from the present moment.

Even when I was present I often was not emotionally available because I regarded my heart as a nuisance. It always got in my way and weakened me with its emotional demands and needs. Its anger was troublesome and I was convinced I needed to squash it. Its need for belongingness, tenderness and affection were beyond comprehension to me and very threatening to consider. There were more important things to think and worry about than what was going on now. You have your own story of drifting away from the present moment.

**One of the first deep discoveries in interim places is that your fear and desire are always about the future.**

Consider the possibility that you live primarily in the future as I have, and only seldom—and not for very long—inhabit your actual life today. Your actual life, the only life you really have, only takes place now. When you feel afraid, it is about some imagined future catastrophe. If something goes wrong in a work project you fear this in part because someone *will* find out and conclude that you are inept. When money becomes an issue in a business downturn, or when health problems arise, you are actually afraid of the day soon coming when all cash reserves or health and life itself *will* be gone and then you *will* certainly be in trouble! When there is trouble in your relationships you imagine where it *could* lead and what you *will* have to do then! The future robs us of our life today.

I always seemed to have what I required in the actual moment of *now*. I seldom feel afraid of the actual present moment I live in. I feel alive in it. This is likely true for you, too. You have made it this far so you must have a good sense of how to get by.

You cannot live with permanent fear and obstruction. Your body and heart are not designed for this. Interim places teach a severe lesson: be present to the one life you are given today or die.

Be present or die from fear and the ravages that fear brings to our fragile bodies. Or die from the disappointment of not having gotten all that you think you needed from your future. You become more interested in the present only when your future creates too much desperation for you to continue to hold onto. The present moment, always and in every circumstance, is your only place of rest, the only place of real excitement and creative challenge, and the only place in which the spontaneous life of your sacred self finds expression. Sometimes this happens in surprising ways.

I decided to run a half marathon in my hometown. Lisa and my daughter, Cate, came to watch. I was clear about the finish time I set as a goal and chose to have fun and feel good about my effort throughout the race. Eight miles into the thirteen-mile race I felt more tired than I should. I felt strangely afraid, too. I felt I had fallen short of my goal. I tried running harder but simply felt more tired. Then, from my depths, a voice spoke to me. It simply said: *'Run the race that is in you to run.'*

I immediately wept with joy. I felt instantly lighter and clearer about what I wanted to do at that moment.

**This voice of the sacred self always has the impact of lightness, clarity and release to it.**

I finished better than I have ever finished a half marathon and recorded my best time. One minute under the goal I set for myself.

From that moment on, I began to see that the essential question each day is, "What is in me to do today?" This is not a plan as much as it is a question that allows your essential nature space to move and flow within you. You will frequently be surprised by what is in you to do. As you learn to turn and face this question each day peacefulness becomes possible because you have acknowledged you are alive only in this present moment. All other moments are illusions; they may or may not arrive. All moments, the good and bad, come and go like passing clouds, as the Buddhists say. Your task in the present is to be grateful for being alive. It is a gift.

Life certainly is a better option than any other option you know about. Whatever catastrophe you imagine has not yet happened in this moment. There is reason for both rest and celebration only in today, in this present moment.

You release joy as you accurately assess what you have now and find thankfulness in your hearts for this. This is not always easy because we have a strong tendency to scan the future and then frighten ourselves when we discern a threat that we then begin preparing for. I am like Jesus' disciples who watched and helped him break two fish and three loaves of bread to feed five thousand people (and then gather together the leftovers!). Yet just two days later they worried about how and where they would eat. With me, God is only as good as His next glamorous miracle. Day by day, we learn to rest in the present.

## ❯ Embrace opposites as a way to bring balance

Good and bad. Light and dark. Hope and despair. Love and fear. Birth and death. Change and stagnation. Faith and faithlessness. Your life is full of opposing tendencies. You want to live fully and contribute in the best possible way and, at the same time, you shrink back from this stance and doubt even the most valid assessment of your gifts and abilities. Both aspects are true; anyone who claims to know you would be able to report on both parts: the passionate, lover of life and the coward. Interim places rock us loose from our fixed views of ourselves, our either/or places of judgment and expose us to paradoxes that only the heart comprehends. If you want more balance in your life, look inside where you are out of balance first.

The open heart knows these are not opposing forces at all but rather variations of the full range of expression available to each of us. What prevents us from tasting more of the full range of behavioral responses is our judgments about what's good and bad, right or wrong for us. You loosen your grip on the fixed view of who you are and what's okay one painful finger at a time. One guest house visitor at a time.

Several years ago I worked with the *Center for Creative Leadership* in their *Executive Leadership Development*

*Program.* We'd give workshop participants a battery of instruments and psychological assessment tools as part of the pre-work. As the five-day program unfolded, we shared and discussed results. Invariably, many people would discover information about themselves that was inconsistent. They would ask questions like, "How can I be both:

> *Decisive and indecisive?*
> *Harsh and approachable?*
> *Remote and supportive?*
> *Controlling and delegating?*
> *Quiet and too talkative?"*

They would argue that the presence of contradictions and inconsistencies rendered the instruments invalid. I argued it meant they were human. I knew I was full of contradictions myself: sensitive and abrasive, yielding and controlling, accepting and intolerant, engaging and remote, influential and nearly invisible. Interim places later exposed me to opposing forces I needed to embrace so my heart could be opened and remain open to my life. The disorientation of interim places requires a new sense of balance that you gain by learning to hold opposing tendencies, opposing ways of living, as equally valid.

You enter interim places wanting simple answers right away. Instant clarity, instant cash flow. Instant and permanent peace and joy. What you actually experience is how extraordinarily complex you are. How vastly intricate and confusing you can be. How challenging it can be to navigate through the numerous voices that glide like storm clouds over the surface of your mind each day, impermanent visitors in a large kingdom. You slowly become interested in this vast internal kingdom with its impossible opposites. Rilke[4] wrote the following piece in the early twentieth-century:

*Whoever grasps the thousand contradictions of his life*
*pulls them together into a single image,*
*that man, joyful and thankful,*
*drives the rioters out of the palace,*
*becomes celebratory in a different way,*
*and you are the guest*
*whom he receives on the quiet evenings.*
*You are the second person in his solitude,*
*the tranquil hub of his talking to himself.*

The contradictions and paradoxes revealed in the times of unbidden silence and solitude were, to Rilke, an important part of our life to comprehend. There is a joy and thankfulness in embracing paradox that gives way to a celebration different from all others. Up until now you may have felt that only certain qualities of yours were valid and worthwhile; others you judged as invalid, shameful even. The competent, rational, successful and productive aspects are fine; the, lazy, unorganized, slow, dumb, awkward aspects are another story!

Perhaps the *rioters in the palace* are those aspects of you that spring up violently and uncontrollably because you have not acknowledged or embraced them earlier. Only as you embrace the many contradictions within do you move closer to compassion, the gift of an opened heart. I continue to have qualities that are like wild, untamed horses in me. I do not know when they will appear except that they typically cause pain to others when they do. While I regret the impact my behavior has on others during these moments, I no longer try to corral the wild horses. They're just aspects of me that are not tameable; I keep an eye on them and put them in a guest room down at the end of the hallway, away from the others. I take them for occasional walks at my own pace and in my own timing.

I want the single image without the contradictions, just like my students in the *Center for Creative Leadership*. The resurrection without the crucifixion. The image of yourself as a single unified personality is the most difficult image to let go of. You live and work in a culture that only wants and values the high ground of reason, logic, clarity and order. Not the messy ground and tangled terrain of interim places. The trouble is, turbulent waters of change everywhere are the breeding ground of these deeper wellsprings of spirit. You cannot downsize, layoff, restructure and merge, divorce, raise children, drive hard for results, and do all the other things on your calendar without simultaneously unearthing the fear, hope, and disorientation of deep change in yourself and others around you.

Each of these sets of opposites speaks to basic ways in which the universe works to open us to the balance of masculine and feminine forces of the heart within. We need, over time, to develop competency in the full range of behaviors contained in both ends of the continuum.

## ❯ *Grasping and releasing*

We have spoken of the need for surrender. In real ways, surrender is one end of the continuum around an attachment. Grasping is the other end. There are times where it is good to grasp tightly. When a child is sick and timely medical action is required, it makes sense to create a timetable for action and ensure all appointments are kept, all advice is acted upon, and all medication taken as prescribed. When in actual physical danger, it makes sense to do what's required now and not waste valuable time and energy squabbling over small matters that only splinter the concentration required for survival. In these situations where a prescribed course of action must be followed to the letter, it is wise to hold on tight to the process required for a return to health and safety.

When in deep change and transition, however, grasping can have just the opposite effect. You will grasp onto any strategy that will keep you safe or return you to safety. You want only to be out of danger and it does not matter if the danger is real or imagined. Fear is always real. You scan the landscape of your life and develop a fixed map of what threats exist and plan how you will move through the obstacles to get what you want. You're no longer responding to life but rather reacting to your fear.

In most organizations, this passes for good management. Strategic planning is, after all, an assessment of threats and opportunities and managers are encouraged to work hard and fast to 'get their arms around' the factors at play.

**We grasp onto things which help us find pleasure and avoid pain, and release only after exhausting ourselves with grasping.**

As I write today I scan to see where I have billable days and how much income I can anticipate for upcoming expenses. When I pray, I direct my grasping prayers towards imploring God to respond to me in tangible ways that I can see and understand. I am addicted to my need to know. I grasp familiar ways and means. I close myself off from other developments that might take place if I could loosen the death grip I have on myself.

Rilke knew that deep surrender or release comes in the cauldron of deep turmoil where nothing short of the death of the old self is at stake. Something new and greater may well emerge but, right now, it is not knowable. This place of suffering attracts spiritual powers and capacity in ways that no other human experience does. A drowning person doesn't care if their cries carry some mystical meaning; they want to live. But they cannot be saved when they're fighting and struggling for their survival; a wise lifeguard moves in only after they have stopped fighting.

You release your grasp first and then surrender what has been released to the sacred. Releasing comes when any and all solutions to your struggle are okay with you; you grasp at none, you reject none.

Sometimes you drown.

That's the harsh news. Releasing your grasp on life does not bring a guarantee of wealth, health and happiness. If it did, they would teach it as a required course in business school. Releasing is difficult because you only approach it when all other strategies have failed and when what's at stake matters deeply to you. My own struggle in interim places has been about money and success, about my identity as a man, a father and contributor to this planet. I have needed to release all definitions of myself because they became too heavy a burden to carry and kept me from seeing how magnificent I really am! You have by now undertaken a similar shedding of outdated baggage you no longer need to lug around.

When grasping fails to give you the desired results, you first feel anemic and helpless. You project the rage you feel at your own helplessness onto God (and onto others). Rilke wanted an engagement with the sacred in the midst of this fire. He knew his grief was great and important and offered it to God. It was not something to get rid of, to move away from, to annihilate. He did not want to fix his grief. He knew he was at the end of his rope and discerned that, even in this place, he was not truly alone. *There was a presence other than his own intellect and personality even there.*

This is what he wanted to engage.

**Interim places are great moments in our lives where we are led to the edge of a deep abyss and asked to let**

**go of the things that will weigh us down us in the future where lighter travel is required.**

Your open heart requires you to learn how to surrender. You cannot grasp your life tightly forever without incurring great damage from the universe and from your own body and relationships. It is too lonely an experience, too exhausting. Grasping separates you from your heart.

All of the great religions speak of the human tendency to hold tightly to the small life we mistake to be our own while losing sight of the abundant life that truly awaits us. The trouble is: We love our small life. We love our work and the resources it gives us. We love having enough of what we need. We love the respect and admiration of friends, clients and colleagues. We love being seen as good and decent people. I love the relationship I have with my daughter and with my partner, Lisa. I loved my health. I loved being purposeful and clear about what I contribute to this world. I loved having a vision and seeing myself move towards it each day.

These are good things. We each grasp at our life when any of these are threatened.

You surrender only when you know you must and then only reluctantly. You and I are the swan in another Rilke[5] poem which speaks of surrender:

**THE SWAN**
*This clumsy living that moves lumbering*
*as if in ropes through what is not done*
*reminds us of the awkward way the swan walks*
*And to die, which is letting go*
*of the ground we stand on and cling to every day*
*is like the swan*
*when he nervously lets himself*
*down into the water, which receives him gaily*

*and which flows under and after him,*
*wave after wave*
*while the swan, unmoving and marvelously calm,*
*is pleased to be carried, each moment,*
*more fully grown, more like a king,*
*farther and farther on.*

Your experience in interim places is a story of your love for the ground you stand on and cling to each day! Only as you release your grip on your work and life and surrender to a greater unknown will you taste the fullness of living, the blessings of wonderful relationships, the freedom of living abundantly without undue emphasis on the future. The grace-filled rest that only comes from stepping into each day as an adventure without first needing to evaluate or understand is one of the great gifts of partnership with your sacred self.

Even when you hate the ground you stand on you may still cling to it. At least it's familiar to you! You cling until you're exhausted from clinging. The beauty in "The Swan" poem is that after the swan leaves the safety of the shore, he is received gaily and strangely carried along, growing into a king! Though surrender is terrifying, you are asked by the sacred to surrender to something greater. Grace, synchronicity. It may take many different forms. But, you will not know this while standing on the shore. You discover grace by stepping off the familiar shore into the deeper water of your own life.

As your heart opens, you discover that what you really want is:

- ➤ Awareness you joined in union with your creator.
- ➤ To know you are safe here and that you belong here.
- ➤ To know you have the capacity to experience and respond to your life.

➤ To remember who you are and why you came here and then live this life!

Initially, only the presence of something great can cause us to surrender. Either great suffering or great vision. Your sacred self has brought you to the point of turmoil with no escape route and then invites you to surrender. The sacred self knows that to truly experience the love and joy of creation, you need to release the tight grasp you have on who you are and what you call real life. The sooner you learn the better. *Say yes quickly!*

Rilke[7] begins his great poem of surrender with the words, *"It is possible* that I am pushing through solid rock . . ."* Even the word *possible* can crack the concrete slightly when it rolls out of your wild mouth. Even the smallest of cracks in how you view your life can bring into your experience a wonderful spaciousness. Spaciousness shifts my relationship with fear. In one instant I have a perspective, a distance from it: *It is possible that there are solutions I have not yet seen . . .*

You begin to notice a hidden sweetness in tough times. There are small traces of loneliness and sadness that lay blossoming in the shadow of your fear like winter flowers with beautifully soft aromas you have never smelled. A sweet joy that lies underneath the sharp tooth of fear. You begin to notice the many small things that go well each day, the moments of grace and serendipity that abound like wild flowers on the side of a mountain. The utility bill that is lower than you thought it would be. The especially friendly clerk at CVS. The refund check from the IRS! The rain that stops just as you get out of the car to walk into the post office. The soft pink light just before sunset. *Tasting all of these things and letting them have their way to waken me, I shiver and resolve: In my life I will more than live.*

When you surrender you cultivate a radically different life stance in this world. You come to see that your inner divinity, your sacred self, (the core part of who you are that is beyond all the constellations of personalities, qualities, habits, strengths and weaknesses), is greater and more magnificent than anything that can happen to you on this earth. You are, in your essence, greater than your accomplishments, greater than your struggles, more than your shortcomings and beyond all hard times. You are none of these things but rather greater than the sum of them all.

Release and surrender are the gateway to the central place of the sacred self. True surrender is the destination in the unbidden soil of interim places.

## ❯ *Forcing and allowing*

A sabbatical in interim places brings to an end the fierce active part of you that only pushes forward. It kills the immature warrior in you that only knows one movement: straight ahead now. When you're lost, this kind of frenetic activity will get you more lost and can bring about real danger. Being lost requires a different kind of action, more powerful, to emerge.

In our western culture there is a premium placed on the value of direct action: it's seen as the only way to get anything done in your life. When things go awry, it simply means you need to work harder, try harder, put more time and energy against it. Moreover, to be a good man or woman, a good worker, or a parent and provider means consistently doing good work somewhere and getting things done. On the other hand, there are miracles and by now you have seen that the universe seems to respond to people who, through prayer and meditation and surrender, can appeal to un-seen forces in times of need. You have faith but prefer direct action.

You have passed through dark moments that have gone on for many months in interim places where there was no path to be seen. And God seems to disappear, leaving no presence or footprints to the left, right, behind or in front of you. You have felt abandoned and lost, jettisoned out into space by some satellite that previously was your life but which moved on without you. In this circumstance you may want to do anything to force safety and belongingness to return. Some people race at this point, with short term action that relieves them of the present uncertainty and pain. It is understandable that you want more than anything to react now and to do something. At least you can feel in control of something!

It is the worst thing you can do.

Doing anything from this place of fear only spins you deeper into the quicksand of your fear. You may buy yourself a few minutes or days of temporary relief but all that has really happened is you have allowed your fear to drive you to action. At some level you have come to know this now. You know that when you react you make your fear bigger than you are. Deliverance here lies in embracing the opposite of forcing.

*You allow what wants to happen to happen.*

*Allowing is what you do the moment after you surrender.*

It is the absolute last thing that you can imagine doing that would bring you the comfort you seek. You say another rough prayer, breathe deeply many times. There are no vows, no deals and no pleas in this spot. Only silence and stillness. You do nothing.

**"Not doing" is an active stance; it is not for the faint of heart but for those whose heart is opening.**

You do nothing in a very different way. You do so with attentiveness, awareness and trust, but with no attachment to any particular next steps or contingency plans. In this moment of allowing, there is no escape for you, remember? Summon your heart, quiet yourself, breathe and allow the next moment to come to you as it alone can. Allowing is fierce action and requires courage, patience and confidence in your expanded self.

This is a place in the path of your life where *who you are* at this moment is far more important than *what you do.* Because this is so, you can do nothing and still accomplish everything that needs accomplishing. Doing nothing involves several things. Your process may look something like this:

1. First, you are alive in this moment so tell yourself the news and announce your gratefulness. Out loud.

2. Next, tell yourself exactly what the current reality looks and feels like to you right now. Out loud. Begin this by stating, "Right now I am telling myself this . . ." Next, acknowledge your feelings about these circumstances, all of your feelings, i.e., "I feel *grateful* for my breath and health, *concerned* about this morning's breakfast meeting with the client that did not go well, *angered* that the car repairs are going to be far more expensive than planned for, and perhaps *stuck* with how to proceed with a new project."

3. Invite your sacred self, God / Spirit / The Universe to move into and through this situation in any way they want, doing what they want.

4. Go on your way and do something else that is in you to do at this time. All the while, however, pay attention to what happens around and in you. The skill here

is to contain your concerns without getting caught up in them; bind them in your heart and move on, knowing the matter is still unresolved. Hold the "unresolved feeling;" don't ignore or deny it. Notice any thoughts, ideas, new ways of looking at the matter, new ways to break out of old boxes.

## ❯ *Balancing not doing with action*

**Intimate relationships:** Our anniversary had come and gone with both of us traveling for work projects. We agreed to treat ourselves to a nice dinner at an exclusive restaurant. I noticed I felt anxious about this rendezvous. I wanted very much for the evening to be intimate and engaging, a time for both of us to reconnect after many days of being away from each other. So how do we get started? I invited my sacred self to assist. The next day I noticed small pads of paper on the hotel desk. I immediately sensed that I could is take small pieces of paper and write intimate questions on each one. Then, at dinner, we could surprise ourselves by drawing questions and finding our way into a wonderful dialogue. This is exactly what happened! An absolutely delightful evening that we still talk about!

**Home & auto repairs:** Numerous instances where there appeared to be major engine damage (oil leaks, broken hoses, and fluid puddles), electrical outages and potential water damage that ultimately, after they were released, became inexpensive troubleshooting moments or incidents that happened virtually in the parking lot of a service station where repairs were quickly made. The perfect home showed up for us, another home was sold for cash, with virtually no effort on our part, at the right moment that we needed these to happen.

**Work results:** Numerous instances where conflict with difficult people and groups was averted by surrendering myself and all parties to spirit beforehand and seeking engagement, truth telling and deep resolution of issues. Results: surprising authenticity, vulnerability and a willingness to engage tough issues including our own complicity in the problems we came to discuss. Healing of individuals, relationships and teams.

**Cash flow and income:** Numerous instances where new income came in just as it was needed from surprising sources. Periods of low supply were met and moved through with ease.

**Health issues:** Several instances of breakthrough healing where none seemed possible. Addiction arrested, cycles of dependency interrupted and confidence restored for the personal work that will need to go on for a lifetime. Other times, emotional trauma of several people was greatly reduced in the midst of significant health crises, leading to a sustained ability to face tough issues more authentically, more compassionately with less stress.

**Allowing is easier when you know you have no control anyway!**

The stance of not doing is essentially a stance of allowing your life and sacred essence to do what they want. After all, you have been brought to a standstill because your life has decided this is what it wants for you. Perhaps something better will emerge or perhaps it won't. In this moment it really doesn't matter. This way of being in relation to your life is one of cultivating, slowly and patiently over time, a relaxed grip on your own life. You do not have to talk yourself into believing anything about your future, only allow this moment to happen like it wants to happen.

# ❯ *The author is still alive!*

Another example of balancing timely action with non-action over time. As of this writing I am still alive. All that once seemed lost has been restored. I have a new home, a new intimate partner in Lisa, a vital relationship with my daughter, new clients, and much more confidence in my own capacity. This small acknowledgement of my current reality might amuse you but I have lived through days that I was convinced would be my last. So have you. I was convinced I would lose everything that mattered to me. So were you. The stance of doing nothing has opened a critical space through which much light and grace now flow. The same is happening to you, or you would not be attracted to this book.

You stand and deliver. It is deceptively powerful when you stand in the middle of crisis, breathe deeply, and be still. I have personally experienced financial breakthroughs that I hadn't noticed before while in this stance of allowing. I have had entire strategies for projects drop into my consciousness with such clarity that all I had to do was copy down what I was seeing and hearing. I have found ways through difficult relationship obstacles with people by slowing down, doing nothing, and paying close attention to everything that came into my mind during that time. Ideas, strategies, simple ways through tough dilemmas. Wisdom invariably shows up, sometimes in amusing ways. A way through appears. 'Allowing' is a powerful stance.

The forcing-allowing dynamic is a supreme test of character and a deepening of your own humanity. To come through this passageway may take a minute or a month or several months or years. You may feel like you fail a hundred times and it does not matter. We move in small steps and even a tiny, imperceptible shift yields results. At some point, you sense that even though similar crises have floored you in the past, you now are able to meet them in a grounded confidence, knowing that you have the capacity to handle things.

## ❱ *Move ahead by standing still: when nothing appears to happen, everything happens*

Americans are a people who value movement and change. We admire those of us who move forward against great odds and overcome great obstacles to claim the prize at the end. The prize is invariably some tangible material of considerable worth: a house, a business venture, a vacation, a car etc. Or something less tangible, i.e., a successful, ascendant career. In my work with corporations I see where others and I have played out this incessant drive to keep moving forward in ways that often become addictive and self-destructive. Move fast, move often, don't stand still are trademarks of our culture. The soul of an organization, and our own spirit as well, can be crushed in the rush for quick success.

The trouble is that moving fast and often means living and working superficially. Only those items that can be seen and discussed while we move at 100 mph are considered valid for discussion at all, around either the dinner table or boardroom. You know this by now: the deeper issues of the heart and soul go unrecognized and are not considered important to delve into. Most failed efforts to change in marital and organizational transformation are linked to these deeper issues that we do not reflect on until it is too late, if even then. We're too busy with more important things. Interim places interrupt the preoccupation with speed.

Interim places are the soul's surgical strike into areas of your heart and psyche that can only be reached through stillness and reflection, the absolute last thing you choose for yourself. This kind of unbidden stillness unfortunately accompanies loss of some sort. It is of little consolation that one of the great transformative disciplines in virtually every spiritual tradition is *stillness*, i.e., "Be still and know I am God." Your capacity for stillness is born from your experiments with letting go of the past and future, turning to face now, and balancing your drive for results by releasing and allowing God's light into difficult matters.

## ❱ *Surface fears, deeper calm: living gracefully with what is unresolved*

It is early in the morning. I sit out on my front porch writing morning pages. It is a beautiful spring morning, cool and sunny, with a crisp breeze blowing through the trees. I am two days away from my fiftieth birthday. I make the following entry in my journal:

"So beautiful out here today. So very beautiful. It has taken me many years to enjoy, once again, the beauty of the earth that I knew so well as a young boy. To be able to sit here in peace, amidst all the on-going uncertainty of my life, and enjoy the moment with its resplendent beauty. Is this what interim places is all about?"

You slowly come to the realization that during this time when, to your eyes, nothing appeared to move forward, your heart knew that *everything* is happening. Your heart has opened. Even with things unresolved, you feel alive and more whole than ever before. Your relationships have become more real, more human because there is more of you in them now. Most importantly, the space within you that was so tight and guarded for so many years feels more spacious now, bigger, wider than before with fewer fences and boundaries.

# ☽ *Tools for the Journey*

**Ways to continue opening and trusting your heart:**

➤ Be gentle with yourself during this time of transformation; you will see many aspects of yourself which may shock, embarrass and confuse you. Suspend judgment as best as you can. Your entire repertoire of competencies is being deepened and expanded.

➤ Stop all comparisons between you and others today. Right now. Comparisons create suffering. The life you live is unique from all others. Live it like nothing else matters.

➤ You're outgrowing the small boxes in which you've kept your gender identity. You can still be a good man even when you allow things to happen with being at the helm driving action. You can still be a real woman when you're in charge, directing action or doing other things for yourself.

➤ Do little things each day that bring you joy. This is a demanding discipline and a skill worthy of development.

➤ Make one contact with and observation of nature each day: Yesterday, a mourning  dove sat just over my shoulder on the telephone wire and sang her song; I felt lonely and called my brother. Keep an awareness of the larger community around you.
Appreciate its beauty.

➤ Find a moment for expressing your gratitude on a regular basis.

# ) *The Sacred Self observes*

*You have wanted abundance of life on all levels, dearest one, and this life stance is essentially a stance of opening the heart to the beauty of each moment. All things that you have desired will be yours in their time because this is the way of things. Your intention and choices do matter, but how your life comes to you is in the hands of Spirit. The deeper work of loosening your grip on attachments to various illusions of identity is a most difficult and challenging task for humans. Many people, perhaps even most, do not undertake it at all unless forced to. Even then, the journey involves so great an experience of loss and death that it is easily abandoned at any positive turn of events.*

*You have stayed true to this deeper work. As you enjoy the fullness of beauty here this morning you are also receiving part of your gift back from spirit: the gift of peace and assurance that you are not here alone but rather are part of an extended community of love and reverence with capacities for change, growth, healing and transformation that are far greater and deeper than imagined.*

*The heart that is open in gratitude to simple beauty can receive the things of the world without grasping or clutching. The heart that misses beauty, doesn't see it, and does not know the joy of quietness and stillness will grasp at anything exciting, grand and stimulating. This is simply the way of the world and the way of ego in the world. "If I can become big enough, and great enough, if I build, succeed, acquire and become successful enough then I will surely be safe and secure. I will become worthy." This is not the way of Spirit. Now you know. You are worthy. You are loved. You are held. You are safe. You belong here. Each of these statements are true simply because of who you really are.*

*Everything you need you have within you. Everything you want accomplished is already in you in its finished form. All of nature speaks to you continuously of the way things really work: sparrows tell you of abundant food and building supplies; the oak trees tell of sturdy growth through many challenging and turbulent seasons, across many generations; the rivers speak of the need for fluid movement bounded only by the riverbank of your imagination. The scent of spring flowers, the smell of autumn hayfields, the endless beauty of the dawn and dusk light that shows in the sky all speak to you of the need to balance a preoccupation with the demands of your life with the need to rest and drink in the beauty of creation. The heart that is opened is fed by beauty, nourished by a sense of belongingness to this beauty and celebrates most when it accurately sees and rests in proper relationship within the community of beings. You are one of many beings who make their home here, dearest one, along with the trees and waters, rivers, insects and animals, stones and plant life.*

*Communication is abundant on all of these levels to the heart that is opened and attentive. You and those who read these words have learned the discipline of stillness, of paying attention to the small things around you each day. Gratitude has begun to take root in your heart. With these subtle movements in your life, you begin to . . . "more than live."*

# *Oceans*

*I have a feeling that my boat
has struck, down there in the depths,
against a great thing.
And nothing happens!
Nothing . . . Silence . . . Waves . . .
Nothing happens? Or has everything
happened,
and are we standing now, quietly, in the
new life?*

— Juan Ramon Jimenez[1]

### CHAPTER 9

# The Sublime Gift of Powerlessness:
Opening the strange doorway to your purpose, true path and voice.

INTERIM places are about powerlessness. The sacred focus of deep change and transformation is about your relationship with powerlessness. You have wound up in a predicament where you can do nothing directly to bring about your own deliverance or directly alter the circumstances of your life or your loved ones. No Light, All is Lost, No End in Sight, No Escape. This period in your life is about powerlessness and about how to change the way you hold power in your life.

We don't have much knowledge or training in powerlessness. It does not show up on the school curriculum or on the list of required management competencies in your workplace! Even when we greet it face to face, we're usually left feeling like the great poet above describes: we have a instinctive sense that we have struck against something great . . . but nothing happens! Another great poet, Rilke, up against a stone of an obstacle, cannot move but only can stand and surrender. Make no mistake here: you have arrived at this point in your path to learn about powerlessness. This is life changing learning for you, since from your sacred self's perspective, the joy, purpose and authenticity in your life directly swing on your capacity to stand squarely in your powerlessness.

Interim places reveal internal blocks that limit the way you live and work in the world. Instead of living fully and working to your potential (and helping others do the same), you have lived in impoverished ways and scarcely touch what's possible for you. The universe has arranged just the right people and circumstances to show you what now needs to be released. You no longer have to fight them; they are your friends and not your enemies. Often these messengers of healing come in the form of impossible people and frustrating circumstances that bring you to your wits' end. Your old way of being simply cannot go on unchanged if you hope for any breakthrough. A new way cannot emerge until you see, acknowledge and release the old.

## ❯ *Secret openings, hidden doorways: recognizing impossible obstructions as invitations to a new way of living*

We each have our own share of suffering and hardship. During interim places these are magnified for all the reasons we have discussed thus far. There are patterns, however, that are predictable. When you face them directly and walk through them with your sacred self—not alone or under your own power, no matter how great this power—then a new life opens for you.

> ➤ Seeking others' approval and admiration. Your fear tells that you must manipulate others to like you. 'If I ever showed them what I really thought or felt, something horrible would happen to me.' Now you've come to a crossroad and you know you can stay hidden no further; either tell the truth and risk everything or stay hidden and suffer immeasurable loss.

➤ Blending in. Your fear tells you that you must blend in with the group at all costs. If you trust your own wisdom and leadership or express a viewpoint or direction that is different, something horrible might happen to you. Perhaps now you have been thrust out into the deep waters of your own life on your own; there is nobody to help you or watch over you now.

➤ Isolating yourself. Your safety has been connected to remaining aloof and detached. If you amass knowledge, you believed, you could stay on top by knowing more than others. If you became entangled with life and especially with emotions (your own and others'), something horrible will happen to you. What you secretly feared has happened; you are awash in rage, fear, confusion and grief and completely sucked into something that feels both suffocating and yet strangely, timely.

➤ Being invulnerable. You have built a life and career by being strong and invincible at all times in order to be safe and worthwhile. In your mind, you've assumed that if you had any needs or felt any vulnerability it had to be crushed immediately, or something horrible would happen to you for being so weak. Perhaps now you are hospitalized, or have in some way been rendered helpless and unable to effect change. You are up against a superior force that doesn't seem at all interested in your apparent invulnerability.

➤ Being powerful. Up to this point, you have acted as if you must always be more powerful, more all-conquering than others and secretly feared (only to yourself) that if you let up for even a moment, something terrible would happen to you and to all you have built, amassed or acquired. Now, through a strange set of circumstances you either risk losing it all or you feel dead and exhausted inside, continuing to hold it all in place.

➤ Winning, earning others' admiration and respect. You have always tried to be #1 or at least appear to have your act together. This applies not just to competitive challenges, but to relationships, intimacy, disagreement and/or any demand for new learning. You have never allowed yourself to be a beginner, a learner without needing to be the best out of the gate. Now you find yourself knowing and able to do virtually nothing that makes a difference; you feel overwhelmed and frightened and fearful of what others would say if they knew.

➤ Being perfect. You have been virtually addicted to always performing flawlessly from the start, always in every way. Any mistake opens the door, you have assumed, to something horrible happening.

## ❯ Everything has been perfectly set in place for you: a tight space with no escape

These circumstances may be big and all at once, or smaller and take place gradually over time. What matters is that you know this with certainty in this moment: these are not accidents, unlucky developments, mistakes, or overlooked details. These are signals from the sacred that you are on the doorstep of significant change. There have been other signals before these but you missed them. We have repeated them in this book. No blame. It wasn't time for you to see.

Like the great poet Rilke, you cannot know what is on the other side of the conversation you will not have until you have it. You will not know the freedom on the other side of the imperfection and vulnerability you refuse to acknowledge until you acknowledge these. You will not enjoy the company of unwelcomed guest house visitors— the emotions you turn away from—until you greet and experience them. This *massive darkness* does indeed make you small. You first stand still, offering only your grief, and trust that the transforming of the sacred will be offered to you in exchange. And then you move.

**Has nothing happened? Or has everything happened?**

Initially, it may appear that nothing but more trouble happens when you walk through your powerlessness. The external circumstances may not immediately shift and this will have to be fine. But you have relaxed your death grip on circumstances and you have bellied up to the reality that there is no quick escape. Seeing the subtle changes with your heart, not your eyes, you begin to notice small but significant changes in yourself and in how you stand in relation to the impossible dilemmas above.

## ❯ *It happens without warning yet requires practice: your heart opens*

➤ In place of seeking approval and pleasing others you begin to be able to please yourself. You say what is on your mind and make choices for yourself. You have no need to argue or persuade or change anyone with your actions. You start to get clear on what matters to you and start taking care of your health and life.

➤ In place of blending in you begin to stage small experiments for yourself where you do things that bring you joy. When you get quiet, you listen for ideas of what you can do today without needing others' permission and you proceed to do this. Over time, the whole idea of seeking permission seems worth looking at and you do this too. You begin to authorize yourself to have a life and, with your sacred partner, make this your main agenda each day. Even though you feel selfish some days, you notice that when you save yourself (nourish, safeguard, develop, care for), you and many others seem to benefit!

➤ When you slowly emerge from your granite castle and open your heart, you appreciate how rich and magnificent you are. You're not empty but very, very full. Because you have grappled with your emotions and realized how unpredictable they can be at times, you allowed space for them to simply be in your life without always analyzing and judging. You become your own book, your own source of expertise on how fragile and wonderful life is. You still enjoy solitude, yet no longer feel isolated from others. You cultivate a detached compassion for others because you know what they are up against; you see the same contradictions and hypocrisies in yourself.

➤ When you give up acting as if you are invulnerable you make a startling discovery: people are drawn to your humanity, the very thing you kept hidden all of these years. The exhaustion and weariness you once felt seems to lift and you have more energy. Because you are more open, people open more of themselves to you. At home and at work, things begin to shift. Most of the time this feels a little scary to you and you're still not sure what it means.

➤ On the other side of your need to be powerful, to be in charge, and to lead wherever you are, you begin to notice how willing others are to step up once you move aside. You feel bored and restless and aren't sure what to do with yourself if you're not the leader on the horse up in front. Because you have faced the limits of your power and willfulness through surrender and release, you become less judgmental of yourself, less demanding.

You see how much of your drivenness in the past has been to prove something, i.e., *"I am worthwhile and lovable,"* to yourself and others. This is a bottomless hole in your heart and no amount of building, acquiring, overcoming, merging or controlling will satisfy. You gain humility and perspective. You begin to discern what really matters to you and to others and commit yourself, in new ways, to creating this.

➤ As winning and earning other's respect and admiration loses its grip on you, you first realize how exhausted you've been in trying to measure up. It is terrifying to acknowledge your ragged, unfinished, slow and retarded qualities. This process leaves you very tired for a period of time. Slowly, amidst the old voices, a new voice emerges that you glimpse as your own. You begin to construct your unique life and persist, even when to do so requires that you live for long periods of time with things unresolved and unfinished. Solitude, once your enemy, becomes your friend. You begin to sense that you have much help in this life, both seen and unseen, human and non-human. You have experiences wherein you feel marvelously full and wondrously at one with how things really are.

➤ Perfection carries within it the seeds of knowing what's important and worth doing well and what isn't. You begin to face your terror that not everything deserves endless hours of checking and evaluating or flawless execution. You cultivate perspective. Instead, you reserve your gifts for those aspects of your life where, with a few wise questions and inquisitive prodding, you can help others see what's possible.

Your judgments have practically killed you; they have certainly damaged those closest to you. Leading with your humbled heart, and the companionship of your sacred partner, you begin rebuilding, taking many rests and enjoying yourself in ways that seemed impossible before.

## ☽ Tools for the Journey

**What to do to claim your true power and voice:**

➤ You need only walk through what you fear! But walk through like you have been learning to do through this whole time of change.

➤ Stage small experiments where you can try out new behaviors.

➤ Acknowledge your experience . . . your feelings . . . the impossible sense of it all . . .

➤ Release these feelings and assessments (because, after all, they are just your assessments of what you can see; not the whole story) . . .

➤ Surrender yourself and the circumstances to the sacred . . .

➤ Pay attention, be vigilant but not obsessed . . .

➤ Go about your day and do what is in you to do today.

➤ Be gentle with yourself and know you are not alone.

➤ See this as a time for your transformation even if you're terrified and want none of it. Ask what you need to see or learn.

➤ You don't have to do this time flawlessly; commit to being present with what happens.

➤ You don't have to undo or make up in one day what took you years to develop. Be patient yet open your mouth and speak about what you know. Trust your inner voice to know when and what to do or say.

➤ Remember, you have stood and faced terrifying things during this period. Your capacity for courage, for landing on your feet, is much greater than you may realize.

## ❯ *The Sacred Self observes*

*What is so exciting about this journey of yours, dearest one, and about the journey of those who read these words now, is that you are opening to a great secret: Spirit needs you just as much as you need Spirit. As powerful as you once thought we are, we can do nothing without your willingness and allowing. And you can do nothing without our assistance. Sharing both powerlessness and interdependence, we seek one another's face and trust our relationship will grow deep and strong and durable enough to carry us forward together.*

*We say to you that the path to true, interdependent power begins with vulnerability, not strength as you define it. The surrender you speak of opens all doors and yields a simplicity and elegance of action that is impossible to fathom before you walk through the threshold of belonging. Your fear keeps you separate while only your courage to surrender and allow us room to move enables you and us to belong to one another. You taste the elegance and endless resourcefulness which we can bring, and we enter your human experience and taste your magnificent heart and choicefulness. The beauty of this relationship is unsurpassed, its taste so very sweet.*

*There are hardships in each life; surrender doesn't eliminate suffering, but it does help you see clearly the part of suffering you create with your imagination. As you turn then to face your life as it really is, know with certainty that we are in your every breath and each step you take. Learn to stand in the middle and pause, calling us in on your breath and allowing yourself the moment of freedom available only to humans. Only you can stand back, reflect on what is happening and call forth the resources you require. We undertake on your behalf in difficult meetings, conversations, and dilemmas, as well as in celebrations and times of great joy. You have come into this life to taste fully of this new partnership. Now, sit at your table and rest; be gentle with yourself today. Eat and enjoy your wondrous life.*

*The kind of person that merges from interim places can either be more brittle, more arbitrary and fixed in approach than before, or more relaxed, more open to what one wants to happen. It depends on what voice you pay attention to. Interim places are first about your powerlessness. Yet these times are fundamentally about your openness to becoming who you really are and finding your authentic voice. It isn't that the old voices suddenly and forever disappear. It's just that you attend to another voice which you've cultivated by quieting yourself and paying attention to your inner world. This movement inward then allows you to see and move more into the world in a different, more collaborative way.*

*You might be tempted to take your newly emerging life and immediately plunge into action. There is now reason to pay attention, perhaps more than ever.*

*All that is yours will come to you.*

—A Celtic saying

### CHAPTER 10

## The Trappings of Desire
The secrets of engaging early without attachment ·

AMERICANS are taught from the earliest age to desire. The so-called American Dream speaks to the centrality of desire in our culture. We are supposed to want more, and the dominant white culture says if we are industrious, educate ourselves and work hard we can always get more. In interim places your desire has a more troubling and disturbing underside: desire causes suffering.

We have spoken of the desire that comes from our imaginary, ideal self earlier in this book, and how the imaginary self is built around impossible standards of perfection. It fuels itself with endless comparisons to others and to the past and future. There is no room for failure or struggle or even learning. It is very common for the imaginary self to again rear its head as you begin to move beyond the initial trauma of interim places. Your fear has lessened, you find ways to reassemble some pieces of your life puzzle, the general level of uncertainty becomes more manageable. Without warning, you find yourself caught up in a whirlwind of activity as you try to regain lost ground, lost relationships, lost esteem.

When you operate from the imaginary self, desire is an attempt to grasp control over what has been lost and to safely hold what is yearned for. "If I have or become someone else, then I will be safe and loved . . . then I'll be free from danger . . . ," is the siren cry of the ideal self. Underneath the harsh and unreachable demands of the ideal self is a tender, fragile child yearning only to be known, embraced and loved. This aspect is hard to see and appreciate, especially if you've been strong and confident (and aspiring to great things). As you discover your need for love, hidden underneath your desire to have and be more, this *heart knowing* allows you to find a place of compassion for this otherwise hard part of yourself. The seduction of desire is an aspect that is very easy to give in to because *its voice is the voice of your culture.* It is also the cause of prolonged suffering in interim places.

Grasping desire makes you blind to your original song. Desire takes away the spontaneous movement and wisdom of your heart, spirit and body which often know exactly what you need to do long before the intellect will allow it to happen. The intellect wants to evaluate, compare and then believe; the heart knows. The tension between head and heart, grasping desire and spontaneous desire is a lifelong dance which your time in interim places allows you to see more clearly.

A beautiful story that illustrates this tension between the trappings of desire and the spontaneous, full-hearted, creative being of your heart (without desire) is a Japanese folk tale found in Stephen Nachmanovitch's book, *Free Play, Improvisation in Life and Art.*[2] Though perhaps centuries old, its message is as relevant to us today as it was to the aspiring flautist then. We'll pause to assess **secret openings and hidden spaces** as we go along since this story is really about the entire journey through interim places, a landscape with which you are now familiar.

**THE NEW FLUTE**

*A new flute was invented in China. A Japanese master musician discovered the subtle beauties of its tone and brought it back home, where he gave concerts all around the country. One evening he played with a community of musicians and music lovers who lived in a certain town. At the end of the concert, his name was called. He took out the new flute and played one piece. When he was finished, there was silence in the room for a long moment. Then, the voice of the oldest man was heard from the back of the room: "Like a god!"*

*The next day, as this master was packing to leave, the musicians approached him and asked how long it would take a skilled player to learn the new flute. "Years," he said. They asked if he would take a pupil, and he agreed. After he left, they decided among themselves to send a young man, a brilliantly talented flautist, sensitive to beauty, diligent and trustworthy. They gave him money for his living expenses and for the master's tuition and sent him on his way to the capital, where the master lived.*

This journey begins with our young musician attending a concert because he is a music lover. He is touched by the concert and sees his own calling as he listens to and experiences the master. But there is a trap: *How long will it take* . . . The early warning signs of flawed desire: an urgency to short cut the real work of mastery. The young musicians assess who to send and choose a man with the right technical talent and sensitivity to beauty. Interim places quickly expose the limitations of reliance on technical competency or even sensitivity to beauty. Rather, our work has to do with embracing the undercurrent of fear that lies between us and the real mastery of our craft. Fear leads you to the sweet spot of true mastery, takes you into yourself, and surprises you with a gift.

> *The student arrived and was accepted by his teacher, who assigned him a single, simple tune. At first, he received systematic instruction, but he easily mastered all the technical problems. Now he arrived for his daily lesson, sat down and played his tune—and all the master could say was, "Something lacking." The student exerted himself in every possible way; he practiced for endless hours; yet, day after day, week after week, all the master said was, "Something lacking." He begged the master to change the tune, but the master said no. The daily playing, the daily, "Something lacking," continued for months on end. The student's hope of success and fear of failure became ever magnified, and he swung from agitation to despondency.*

The story deepens. Technical mastery soon gives way to approval seeking and pleasing others; even a simple tune is beyond his reach. Soon, all of his original hope is gone. He has entered *No Light* and *All is Lost*. No amount of bargaining or begging with the master works. The student's grasp (need) for success becomes stronger. This is a telltale sign that the imaginary self is present: an urgent, overwhelming "must have or else" desire for something, coupled with the corresponding fear of one falling short.

*Finally, the frustration became too much for him. One night, he packed his bag and slinked out. He continued to live in the capital city for some time longer until his money ran dry. He began drinking. Finally, impoverished, he drifted back to his own part of the country. Ashamed to show his face to his former colleagues, he found a hut far out in the countryside. He still possessed his flutes, still played, but found no new inspiration in music. Passing farmers heard him play and sent their children to him for beginner's lessons. He lived this way for years.*

The intensity of the student's journey has grown much stronger and he seemingly breaks down. There is now *No End in Sight* and he runs away and attempts to escape his pain by drinking. He wants to disappear from his original love. In your own journey, there may well be a place where your original vision is lost, or becomes too heavy a burden for you to carry. You turn away hoping to escape. But your great gift and original song are still within you, hidden and dormant, simmering until another time. Our young flautist continues to play but finds no inspiration; when you're trying to play for someone else, or do what others would do, you, too, become dead inside.

It is also important to note the shame he felt at his struggle, a pain so hurtful that he refused to show his face to those friends who had commissioned him. Shame can immobilize you, freeze you and keep you from reaching out to resources that can help. When you've lost so much of who you thought you are, what is there left to show those who know you? His self-judgment is severe. There is no room for learning here, for being a beginner. And no compassion for himself. Our task here is to feel and let go of shame. Allow ourselves to be beginners. There is a place in your journey where it is entirely appropriate to lose your vision, purpose and passion. Exceedingly painful, but appropriate. Normal.

> *One morning, there was a knock on his door. It was the oldest past-master from his town, along with the youngest student. They told him that tonight they were going to have a concert and they had all decided it would not take place without him. With some effort, they overcame his feelings of fear and shame and, almost in a trance, he picked up a flute and went with them.*

Even though years have gone by and his talent is seemingly wasted, the synchronicity here suggests the presence of his unseen, unacknowledged sacred partner. There is no escaping his true life as you cannot escape from your own life. Our young master agrees to go, *almost in a trance.* Sometimes your spirit guidance has to virtually stop you in your tracks and put you to sleep in order to wake you up!

Most importantly: what we see here is mastery. It is the deeper work of spirit in each of us. We are helped to fall apart so that we might be put back together again, more wonderfully able to give voice to the unique gifts we brought into this extraordinary world, with our solitary life. All we feel and see is the falling apart, the loss of what we desire and have held so close. This part of the journey is not pretty or wrapped in nice paper and ribbons, but it is the work of mastery! It seems held together by tough luck, strenuous effort, perseverance, near overwhelming exhaustion and much grace.

*The concert began. As he waited behind the stage, no one intruded on his inner silence. Finally, at the end of the concert, his name was called. He stepped out onto his stage in his rags. He looked down at his hands and realized he had chosen the new flute.*

An extraordinary moment that he cannot see from his current vantage point is about to unfold. A dream he no longer grasped yet still held loosely unfolds before his eyes, yet all he sees is a new flute in his hands. What was offered once in grief and desperation is received back. All of the anguish, the long nights crying out to an empty sky, the lost friends, the desperate prayers, the bone-deep bewilderment, the self-doubt that crept into his body and had become a constant companion. The dry days in the countryside wondering if anything mattered anymore or ever would. The solitude, a broken heart. This had become all that he knew. And all he can offer to anyone.

It is enough.

The great exchange, perfectly timed by the universe, is his now to receive because only now is he ready to step into and embody his own life. This is the strangely liberating land of No Escape where nothing really matters except fully entering the moment you are in.

*Now he realized that he had nothing to gain and nothing to lose. He sat down and played the same tune he had played so many times for his teacher in the past. When he finished, there was silence for a long moment. Then the voice of the oldest man was heard,*

*speaking softly from the back of the room:*
*"Like a god!"*

Nothing to win or lose. Too tired to run any further, too exhausted to make anything happen, our young master finally found the conditions needed both for his and our own unconditional surrender. The deep work of transformation had brought the young flautist to this moment. Though he wanted mastery, he naturally resisted the disciplines necessary to achieve it. We all do. We have our good reasons, our distractions, our busy lives which we allow to have their way in us until the original desire, for reasons that remain a mystery to us, breaks forth.

You and I travel the same path as the young musician. It may take hours or years; we cannot know. Indeed, this particular journey took years of "study", but study of an entirely different sort than he—and we—signed up for. Only now can the original gift come through. He has gone into his depths and emerged out on the other side. The young musician's story is the story of the mysterious, strangely integrating, terrifying and ultimately transformative work of our essence, our sacred self, in interim places.

# ❯ On the other side of desire: inspired, spontaneous creativity

The open heart is spontaneously creative. It is nimble and responsive. It knows when and how to move and when to be still. It is full of desire to create in this moment and yet is without attachment to outcomes. This is because your open heart has no need to be successful or to prove anything to anyone. Success, after all, only matters here in this lifetime and even then, it is not serenity, it is not belongingness, connection or relationship! It does not earn you any of these things or any particular right standing with God or with your sacred self. The desire for success squeezes the heart and restricts its urge to live fully.

The open heart does not fear failure because failure, should it occur, means nothing more than success. Neither have anything to do with your inherent worth and beauty. The great irony is that if you have advanced this far, you often become more successful in your life, your work, and your relationships because you are less encumbered with the need to be or do anything. You have become less attached to the need to force anything to turn a certain way. The open heart values full living. Success often follows naturally!

# ❯ *Full-hearted living is your single, simple tune*

Beneath all the striving and grasping there is a young and beautiful place hidden in your tender heart; it is your original song, which wants again to belong to you. It has been held all these years by your sacred self. Your journey through interim places—no matter how long you spend here—is your doorway to what's original and essential in your life. It is a time for you to own, reclaim, remember, acknowledge what matters to you when everything else is stripped away. *It is time to run the race and do what is in you to do today.*

Desire that springs forth from your open heart always has a spontaneity, lightness and a joy to it. Fed from within by the sacred self, this desire also attracts vast spiritual power and tangible resources. Prayers to God that originate from this place always get answered because God lives in our sacred self. God is our sacred self, our sacred self is God.

Listen: you will hear direction when you need it, you are given options when you require them, financial resources when you need them. The heart knows this; it's just that the surface noise is very loud. You can know this is true: in the secret still place beneath all the turbulence of your life is a place of rest wherein you are safe, regardless of what is currently happening in your life. Cries that come from this place are always heard because this is a place of connection with and in union with the sacred.

I am coming to understand there is nothing wrong with desire but only with the compulsive tendency we have to attach our identity and sense of safety with it. If we come out of crisis with these same attachments in place, with our heart still closed to who we really are, the crisis has largely been wasted, no matter how much we have gotten through our desire and hard work. We survive, perhaps, but we are more brittle, more cautious about our life and future. We greet subsequent trials and transitions with a closed heart rather than with renewed confidence about our true capacity. I knew this was not what I wanted for my future.

**In every great change or trauma it is crucial to choose early how you want to be at the end, when the period of change is over. Keeping your heart centered on this makes it easier to let go of desire.**

What do you want? Do you want renewed connection with your own divinity and new confidence in your partnership with the sacred? Do you want to test this partnership and see for yourself that you have the capacity to sustain your life—*on all levels*—like you want it to be? Do you want to live your life and not simply occupy the life someone told you was possible for you? Do you want to restore stability in your life and not approach change in a frightened way again? If you answer these questions with "Yes!" a radical openness to experiencing and feeling it is essential. This is the terrain of interim places where the old slips away and the new shows up on the other side of your surrender.

If you have allowed core parts of your ego's desire to die and have experienced essential desire springing forth spontaneously (and sometimes miraculously) from an open heart, then you have experienced something truly beautiful and full of grace from the crisis. If, indeed, you and I need to travel lighter into our future, then an opened heart and proven experience in living and working with the resourcefulness of the sacred self is the only baggage we need to carry. We need not add anything to this mix.

## ❯ *How things really work*

Sometimes, an experience springs from the depths and cracks your current understanding open, like a doorway, allowing an enlightened glimpse at what's real. One evening as I lay on my couch I reflected on abundance and wondered what living a stance of *unattached desire* could be like. This means I have legitimate needs and things that are important to me, but I do not strive and destroy myself or others to acquire or collect them. As I quieted myself, suddenly but with no emotional shift of any kind, I found myself in a trance. I watched as a skeletal ribcage of fear lifted from my chest and hovered over me at a distance of three or four feet. I felt startled and very curious.

I felt surprised first by this surprisingly close, intimate layer of fear. It felt like skeletal armor, a sublime lattice work that surrounded my body and had for as long as I could remember. While I have written much about fear in this book, this skeletal layer of fear was something I had never experienced before. *It was not an emotion but a state of imagined (and therefore real) separation from the sacred.*

When the skeletal structure lifted I felt instantly freer and lighter, as if some weight I had carried for a long, long time had been lifted. The freedom felt exhilarating. I looked up from where I lay and discovered that I was in union with all manner of material things that I wanted in life: money, work, houses and cars, motorcycles and vacations. Intangible things also showed up: influence, contribution and communal impact. I saw things in their essence as energy and sensed that I, too, was the same energy. I felt at one with and very close to all that I wanted in this life.

There was no particular emotion, but rather an overriding sense of connection and belonging. Free from fear and intimately connected to all that I wanted, there was only freedom here; no grasping and protecting, no clinging to anything or even desiring anything. The only proper stance in this place was a stance of open gratitude.

My heart opened and I allowed it to flow into and through me. I immediately knew that striving, trying to grasp, clinging to achievements, guarding my own self and how I was perceived by others in the world, were all unnecessary here. I knew that whatever was truly mine, part of my full experience here in this lifetime, not only would come to me (without my having to force it) but was already complete, fully accomplished and in its finished form. I simply had to open myself and receive.

After several moments passed, the skeletal structure of fear descended down into me again and the trance ended. I immediately felt the sense of separation from the "all that is" that so defines our human experience. Its gravity pull was less now and I knew I could not go back to my previous life stance. I felt full of wonder at this glimpse into another kind of consciousness. I have never lost the memory of what I saw that night. It is the first world from which you and I came!

I realized that much of our striving had been caused by a belief that what we want is a long way away. We imagine it will take a long time to get it or a long period of hard work. Or, if it seems too far, or too big or too impossibly far from our reach, we lose belief in it altogether. Yet, in this vision above: *everything is already here, complete, accomplished, done. There is no striving required or anything for which to strive. The work to be done is learning to allow ourselves to see things clearly and to receive all that we are.*

> **When reduced to energy, you are one with all things and all that you desire exists along with you in its completed form; your move is to allow, not grasp**

This was my first taste of union, the experience of being one with all things. Freedom. Not only was this the world from which we come, it is a glimpse into the future in which you and I now belong. From this place of heart knowing, we now receive and create our life.

## ❯ *Tools for the Journey*

**What to do to remain unattached to what you desire:**

➤ Be especially mindful of those desires that feel urgent and bring you impatience and fear. Ask, "What do I need to learn or see here?"

➤ Notice times when you feel very excited and good about yourself following successful outcomes and how especially low, even despondent you might feel following setbacks. You're continuing to identify with external events in ways that may not be helpful. No judgment here; just pay attention to what happens in you.

➤ Conversely, notice how inwardly steady you've become, how anchored and sure, when your heart has shifted from "I'm good because . . . to I'm good, period." Rejoice here!

➤ Distinguish, wherever possible, the difference between what you want and how to get there. It is easy to become attached to viewpoints and opinions about what is possible. They become small boxes that trap us and hurt others. Stay focused on where you want to end up.

➤ More time, money, personal time, freedom and autonomy all *feel like end results but instead are steps to something else.* What would you do with more time . . . money . . . autonomy, etc.? When you feel delayed or obstructed, kept from what you want, sometimes you're meant to stop and get clear about what matters.

➤ There are, in fact, important things that need to happen within certain timeframes, budgets, etc. Get clear what these end results are as quickly as possible and commit the steps, the doing, the "how to", to your sacred partners.

➤ Pay close attention to those things that bring you joy, that simply bring spontaneous pleasure to you. Notice any patterns: where are you, what are you doing, how are you being and with whom are you doing and being these things when you feel most alive? Do and invite more of these into your life!

> Invent ways and time to be present to the natural world. Take a walk, sit on your porch, listen to the world immediately around you. Watch the ways in which other beings work. The sparrows, wind and summer rain, the creek on the other side of town. Don't think too hard; rather, relax and focus. Ask your sacred partner: "What can I learn here?"

## ❯ The Sacred Self observes

*Dearest brother in the light, we bring greetings to you from the place of oneness within, where we live and move together with you in harmony and union. The path of separation is a path known to all humans, for it is the path you are born into when you arrive here on your beautiful planet Earth. Even naming "Earth" causes us great joy, for she is a place of extraordinary beauty and grace, a radiant star seen throughout the universe. Her light springs forth from the opened hearts of many others who, like you, have begun the journey away from separation into union.*

*Our ability to speak of this place is hampered by your language which, itself, is steeped in the assumption of separation. In truth, you do not move toward union but have access at any moment to the union that always is.*

*This is not a mystery or something available to only the ancient mystics on mountaintops. You experience this union anytime the following experiences happen to you:*

> *a phone call or chance meeting opens up a relationship, activity, or work that brings you great joy;*

> *something you thought would take much effort over*

*time to resolve is completed suddenly with virtually no effort;*

➤ *a conversation you feared would be impossible opens up in front of you and resolves itself, leaving all parties ecstatic and relieved;*

➤ *a physical healing happens spontaneously or, equally important, a way of living through a time of hardship suddenly occurs to you, along with the full knowing of how to do this;*

➤ *others in your core relationship group suddenly make changes in their behavior that bring them, and you, alive with no interference or assistance from you.*

*These are but samples of experiences you and those who read these pages have had. We say to you these are moments of opening when union is clearly visible and accessible to you. It is always present and available; how could it not be? Yet, few reach this part of the journey and we wish to tell you why and what you and others can do about it.*

*First, there is the challenge of seeing through fear, which you have written extensively about here. Fear is triggered when you imagine your identity is bound with external circumstances that always change. They begin and they end. The seed of union, which is at your core, is compromised whenever it is linked to shifting external events. But see this clearly: it is the seed of union trying to push through the soil of your attachments that is at play here. This is why your mystics and poets celebrate the dark invisible workmanship of your life! Underneath all fear, the deeper current of union runs clearly. Your sacred self is this dark invisible worker!*

*Your own path has been an emotional one, dearest brother. It was not time for it to be any other way. Now we say to you to continue cultivating the following actions: surrender, calling forth the fullness of union, opening to receive that which has not been seen yet is known in the secret places of the heart, and expressing gratitude in advance of fully integrating union into all of your life. Each of these actions are ways to accelerate your own journey.*

➤ **Surrender:** Surrender is an act of calling forth the full creative power of your self and the canopy of assistance that surrounds you and every living person. Do this often, beginning with areas of less risk in your life. Pay attention to what happens in those circumstances when spirit has been invoked. Keep notes so you will be able to withstand the logical arguments of the mind. United partnership with spirit is your inheritance. Surrender is the way to actualize it.

➤ **Call forth the fullness of union:** We say to you to speak forth and out loud your intention to remember union. This can be done by remembering that all assessments of current reality are time bound and wrapped in the core assumption of separation: . . . "this will take a long time . . . I don't know when this desired development will occur . . . there is no way this will happen by the end of the year . . ." are common assessments of current realities. We encourage you to add the following affirmations: "Anything can happen at any time . . . there are aspects of this we cannot yet see and they change everything . . . it is possible there is a hidden way through we have not seen . . . we call forth all that is now." This is not a technique. Rather, it is a discipline of putting yourself and those around you in remembrance of who and what you are.

*There are secret openings in times of stress and trauma. There are hidden spaces in all dialogues that can open up new understandings and resolve long-standing tension. Anticipate them, expect them. Keep notes on what you experience.*

➤ **Open to receive what is not yet seen:** This essentially requires cultivating a stance of radical curiosity and wonder, and follows naturally once the actions (above) are taken. The surprising challenge at times will be to allow yourself to receive gifts that drop into your lap.

*The value placed on "hard work and effort" has its origin in an assumption of separation! There will be times when hard work is required; we say open yourself to that which is ready for delivery now!*

➤ **Express advance gratitude:** This action is another reminder to your mind that you refuse to live time-bound to what you can see and hear. The heart alone knows that all things come from the sacred and return to the sacred. All things, therefore, can be celebrated and received as gifts from the sacred regardless of how they appear to our eyes. All things can be received with gratitude.

This action also says (to yourself and others) that although circumstances may appear fragmented, unfinished and undesirable, you know, in the secret places of the heart, that much of what you see is illusion. It may be bad luck, delayed timing or it may be your sacred self at work in ways not understandable to you yet. It doesn't matter. In the stance of union all things are held as complete, even when this completeness is the substance you feel only in the heart. Completeness originates in the unseen world of the heart, not in the external world.

Express your gratitude for all things and for those matters of importance you hold in your heart. Entrust the details of how things will work out to your sacred partners. Gratitude is an expression of confidence (to yourself first and then to us) that you know what has been entrusted and what is returned to you is completely good. Regardless of temporary appearances to the contrary. Gratitude accelerates your transformation and allows you to remain whole and at peace even when circumstances are not yet what you want.

We have said these actions are not techniques and this is so. If you see and use them as techniques you will become easily frustrated when things do not change. When used properly as expressions of the opened heart, you will learn not to attach yourself to outcomes but instead to surrender to what is . . . both what you can see and what remains unseen but known in the heart. You will be able over time to stand firm in your own life as full partner with your sacred self, confident that, between you, full capacity exists to respond to all of your life!

Take these words and wrap them like a blanket around you and comfort those in your life who have not yet passed this way in their journeys. You agreed to remind them of these matters!

**Know we love you as you are. Nothing needs to be added now or ever.**

# The Dream of Now

*You live your life by the light you find*
*and follow it on as well as you can,*
*carrying through darkness wherever you go*
*your one little fire that will start again.*

—William Stafford[1]

### CHAPTER 11

## Moving Forward in The New Partnership
Finding balance, success and abundance in all the
unexpected places.

THERE have been two crises happening at once. One takes place outside of you in the ragged, unresolved, wildly changing and forever unpredictable events of your life. The other unfolds within you, in the secret cathedral of your heart. At this point in your journey you may well have begun to see changes in the external rapids of your life. Or maybe not. It doesn't matter as much anymore. We are conditioned to look outward for indications of significant shifts, not inward where the real shifts occur. The old way in us dies very slowly and with great reluctance! The real shifts have become more visible within and will undoubtedly lead to external changes in time.

We each pass through interim places many times. *Adult life is an interim place* full of endings and new beginnings. Employment, finances and life threatening health dilemmas with a family member have severely tested me as I completed this manuscript. The pages themselves have been a living laboratory in which I have tested and confirmed the concepts written about here. I have seen my way through hardship and have not lost the sacred connection I have shared with you in these pages. There is much for which I am grateful. When you see gratefulness returning to your own lips, this is all the movement you need.

There are several internal shifts that my sacred self has asked me to write about that will encourage and provide direction for you now and in the days ahead. Even though there are no guarantees that your external reality will turn one way or the other, you know that you will prevail, you will go on, regardless. You are spirit and you are one with God, with your sacred self. You live in this world where everything alive has consciousness, everything communicates, everything is connected with everything else. You have endless resources and assistance at your side everyday, all day, without end. In this context, the sacred self and I offer the following indicators of the new partnership taking root and sinking down its roots and extending its branches into every aspect of your precious life.

## ❯ *Detached peace*

*When you are attached in attention and emotion to external objects and externalized things of value, it is difficult to experience peace that endures. When attachments are weakened, peace automatically ensues.* One significant change is that you simply feel more peace and greater joy, regardless of income, work volume and other circumstances you used to worry about. You may attribute some of this to having been through a difficult time and knowing you have what it takes to handle tough times again. Yet there is more to this than just past experience. Something has changed inside you.

You (with your sacred self's assistance) have developed a capacity to live from a deeper place which is not susceptible to the highs and lows of each day. From this place within, you know you are safe and that things will work out. From this sheltered place, you have documented proof of receiving the wisdom you needed to find your way through dilemmas. Sometimes you may miss and actually long for the euphoria you used to feel after an especially noteworthy achievement. You notice the absence of excitement you once felt when you had ideas and proposals accepted, or when respected colleagues admired things you did. You still feel good when this happens but not as wildly good as before. Some days you miss the rush! Don't concern yourself with the absence of excitement: it means you live from a place within that doesn't depend on this for validation anymore.

Many leaders feel restless and somewhat bored after learning how to build a shared vision in their organization. They know it's important, yet they still hunger for the old days when they were directly involved and had their self connected to the outcomes. This longing for the "old rush" feels important to mention because it can be disorienting. I often feel "I'm not really doing anything" on projects and at home, even though much is happening. I feel invested but not attached to outcomes. This is simply part of the learning around detachment. A different kind of involvement follows.

You notice another related shift in yourself: you seldom worry as intensely as you once did or for as long as you did before interim places. There are still things you worry about but now you find your way back to the secret place in the heart much more quickly than ever before. Your physician may confirm this shift: your heart rate, pulse and blood pressure, may have dropped considerably by this point in the path despite more turbulence and change than at any other time in your life. In a real sense, the stance of sacred detachment (surrendering to spirit that which you cannot control) allows you to live well despite many areas where things are not yet resolved. You realize they are already resolved, in the spirit dimension, and that is what matters. You simply have come to see that you cannot and do not need to force circumstances and other people to change.

Again, for those of you who, like me, tend to be worrying types, who look for things to be concerned about, this shift can be disorienting. If you're not worrying, what are you supposed to do? Who are you if you are not the one looking for something wrong to be upset about!

I have consciously followed the path described in the last chapters: experience everything, feel everything, judge as little as I can, surrender everything I cannot control and pay attention within and without for wisdom and other resources. I know I am not alone. And for this I feel grateful. With the absence of continual highs and lows, you begin to cultivate and recognize the emergence of a grounded stance in your life that is not as dependent upon external circumstances. Instead of worry, gratefulness and praise is a good response!

# ❯ The Sacred Self observes

*Peace is your inheritance. In your world torn with violence this statement may seem absurd and so it is to many. Yet we say to you that peace is your right and a requirement for your health and sense of well-being. Fear robs you of peace. You rob yourself of peace any time you attach identity, emotion and self-worth to ideas, viewpoints and causes, regardless of their value. Even so-called righteous people do much harm by imposing their viewpoints on others. The great masters who visit your planet do no operate in this manner, for action taken out of deep attachment creates much resistance, counteraction and conflict. You are light energy beings, not simply biological entities. You will discover that much resistance can be eliminated if shifted energetically, with intention and compassion for all. Detaching from external circumstances is but the first step in learning to live and move more elegantly and simply with your spirit partners.*

# ❯ *Work*

I enjoy my work more than ever and feel I currently do the best work of my life. The most significant shift, however, is that I no longer need to work in order to feel good about who I am. I can walk away from the busyness, the activity and even the achievement and still feel I am of value because of who I am. This way of being was completely unknown to me just a few years ago. It is liberating to locate our own unique value within our essence and not have it tied to the next achievement! Living only for the next achievement is an exhausting way to live. Partnership with spirit promises you a more sustaining and nourishing stance.

The breakthrough occurred when there was no work and no money and I discovered that I was still alive and actually thriving in the midst of this loss. This movement was beyond my rational thought process. Stated another way, when my business was falling apart I did not consciously think to myself "I am more than my work." As useful as that might have been, it was not what happened. *My aliveness was revealed to me . . . that aspect of me that thrives regardless of circumstances was revealed in me to me. I discovered it and was bewildered by it.*

My sacred partner revealed its presence in small ways like this, never with neon lights and television cameras or invitations to appear on *Oprah*. Perhaps, your sacred partner operates the same way in you. We come to see that the release we needed all along is through the very things we fear. As we walk through them, our deep body-soul wisdom is revealed in and to us. We do not advance by will power and force alone; if we are wise, we move forward and expect the universe to move toward us. Our employment and work becomes another venue in which the practical aspects of sacred partnership is manifest.

The sacred self holds the wisdom and resources we need and releases them as a farmer might release seeds at the perfect time. In an instant, we know what we are to do. Looking back, I heard myself tell trusted friends: "My work and life appear to be headed down the toilet but I feel more alive than ever . . . yet I have little to show for or account for this sense of well-being." I know now that all of the maps I used to account for where I am were externally referenced; it was awkward to feel good when external circumstances did not warrant it. *This is a core feature of sacred partnership: peace and resourcefulness in all circumstances.* I felt it first in my relationship with my work and with success itself.

We grow based on what we receive from the sacred and then on what we do and who we become with what we receive. This is not our path alone; we share it with others from whom we receive. We give our *great grief cry* and *receive great transforming* in return. There is a reason I found so little of substance from the self-help books I read during this time in my life: I knew that what I needed had to be revealed in me and I had to receive it. Work becomes a laboratory for experimentation in exchanging things of equal value with spirit: our complex dilemmas for spirit's wisdom; our need for spirit's supply; our fear for spirit's courage; our despair for hope, anger and frustration for the experience of overcoming all that concerns us.

Work may have always been a place where you tested yourself and found out what you were made of. You used your responsibilities to sharpen skill sets so you could advance and take on new challenges. Now, as partner with your sacred self, your role has become larger. Work becomes a place where you test your full capacity—skills and faith, strategies for advancing and accessing your deeper, intuitive wisdom—that tells you when and how to move or whether to move at all. Most importantly, work becomes a sacred place where you continue to strip away your ego-driven designs and allow your sacred essence to direct your activities, relationships and performance.

In time, you begin to sense that you are part of something much larger than your own life and career. You assist in ushering into the workplace a way of being that is grounded in a love which sees the earth as its canvas. What you do affects everything and everyone else. As you lay your concerns, hopes and dreams before your sacred partner, you watch how everything seems to go a little easier for all who are part of your experience. As you seek what is highest and best for all concerned, you begin to witness daily miracles: people say and do things that only a few weeks or months ago would have been unthinkable.

You know you have something to do with all of this but you say nothing because it doesn't matter. All that matters is that you continue to move forward in partnership with your spirit and allow your partner occasionally to remind you of what is truly changing in, around, and through you.

Remember Rumil said: *If you've opened your loving to God's love you are helping people you have not seen and will never know. Our response: Say yes quickly.*

## ☽ *The Sacred Self observes*

*When you are brought to a standstill in your life or work, it is that you might receive input that otherwise would be unavailable to you. Our input often comes in the form of expanded, full-bodied awareness of an issue, or an expanded understanding of your true capacity for responding to life. In your case, dearest brother, you entered wanting to cultivate the consciousness of abundance on all levels. This was your original intent, was it not!*

*We do not teach afternoon classes on abundance! We*

*instead assigned master guides to work with you and usher into your experience a fuller relationship with your essence, your sacred self with whom you write these words. Abundance begins here, is sustained from this source, is resourced and supplied from here, and is received here! We will speak more of this later in these pages. For now, know this with certainty: the great masters (and you are included here even though you resist these words) in all fields are self contained: they are sourced from within from deep wells that do not run dry.*

*No challenge in your work and life is greater than your true capacity to respond. Herein is the secret to rest.*

## ❱ Power

This word either frightens us or excites us. To those who have suffered through the abuse of power by others, the thought of acquiring power of your own may seem upsetting. For others who have grown strong by using power to create what you want, you may feel like we finally are talking about the real stuff of life! For you, power has been about acquiring things of value, about doing well and getting something of value in return. Power has been connected to direct action. The school in interim places reveals a very different aspect of power to each of us, regardless of how we previously felt about it.

Interim places show us that power resides in our consciousness, our presence and being. This kind of power releases when we know who we are (spiritual light beings), remember what we are (a partner with our sacred self), and recognize at any moment that we have access to all the resources we need. The central message is: *I am, in my collective partnership, enough.* Sacred power is born first through humility, then acknowledgement and finally sur-

render. We're only able to move as we move in partnership;
alone we can do nothing.

> ## Doing without doing and getting everything done; balancing masculine and feminine power

Your new relationship with power sometimes requires you
to be very active, doing and building and following things
through to completion. You may be very busy with your
work projects, family and friends. Other times, you may not
be very active or busy at all. You will, as you listen to spirit, do little more than be quiet, read, walk and hang out like
a cat in the sun on a cold day. Your responsibility in relationship to sacred power is to hold light and to hold an energy space that allows what needs to happen to happen. This
is possible to the extent that you remember there is nothing
you need to do or get because it has already been done and
gotten.

Power has to do with your allowing the sacred self to do
what needs to be done and for you to move in alignment with
this part of yourself. The action requires both masculine and
feminine forms of power, balancing allowing and doing.

When I work I actually do less actual facilitating. I say
what is in me to say and then allow my energy to open others up to do and complete the work they have come to me
to do. My conferences, as a result, have become simpler,
more engaging and authentic, more intimate and more
nourishing and liberating for attendees. The "all of me"
which defies description (yet is me and my sacred self) has
its own conscious, creative energy; as I become conscious of
this and allow this energy to work, things go better.

Test this for yourself: the earlier you involve your
sacred self in the substance of your life (your plans,

projects, relationships, courageous conversations that you've had and those you have yet to have), the more elegantly you will move through to the results you want. And, when you don't get what you want, it may be because something even better has now become available and possible. *The house guest you reluctantly invited in has prepared you for some new delight!*

# ❱ *Creating desired conditions beforehand, so we need to react less*

Interim places have taught you that time is an illusion; anything can happen anytime at all. You can now use time to your advantage. As you move in alignment with spirit you can ask spirit to "go ahead and prepare a way through" circumstances you may be concerned about. For example, I set my intentions before a conference, and seek permission to speak directly to the sacred selves of all who will participate in my work that week. I then ask that the energy of all resistance (fear, confusion, anger, misunderstandings) be allowed to dissipate into the Earth. In its place I call forth the energy of love, truth and compassion. I express my gratitude for all that I'm given and open my heart to what wants to happen. This is how I prepare for my work. I have yet to be disappointed by the results! I have come to believe that most of the real work of a conference takes place long before any of us arrive! You have this capacity too.

Work consistently goes much better than ever before; I expend less energy and move more elegantly though my days. I seldom get exhausted anymore, even though I keep a demanding schedule. This kind of power replenishes us and nourishes those around us because it originates in the God-place within, the sacred self or essence, which knows only love. When we move in this power we feel much less stressful, more confident that we've called forth all the resources available to assist us. What more can we do? Our movement (be it activity or stillness) feels effortless. Like a God. When we forget to follow through with this discipline, the work often and immediately feels more difficult and requires much more energy and effort. Experiment with this yourself and build your own experience.

## ☽ *The Sacred Self observes*

*A walk in nature serves as a good reminder of the unlimited, spontaneously creative power of the universe. The seasons change and affect every living being; tides roll in and out again; the animal, plant and insect kingdoms relentlessly pursue what is in them to pursue; vast weather systems move across the face of our beloved Earth and bring both destruction and needed supply. Is not all of this an extraordinary, daily display of true power? In this great dance of power you are but a single being, dearest one. Your plans and dreams, your struggles and suffering are but one part of a very large play!*

*We say this to remind you that true power originates in humility. You are but one of many beings, human and other than human, who have come here to live together. Beyond this recognition of a shared home is your growing awareness that the power to create a life that matters to you is fueled from within where you surrender your life and then receive it back again. These beautiful acts are possible only in a state of humility. Those who claim to be empowered by God and have no humility speak of some other kind of power with which the Earth has grown very familiar.*

*We delight ourselves in you, dearest one, for we know these are not the words you planned to include in this segment on power. These words, however, do describe the power now available to you and to those who read these pages. Open your heart and receive what has been held for you from the beginning. It was not time before this, so do not judge yourself for the time it has taken to arrive here. Go forward as a member of a great community of beings who watch and encourage your movement, and who stand ready to assist as you open to them.*

*Seek our face often, even as we seek yours. There is much love here for you all.*

# ❯ Healing old wounds, recovering from earlier setbacks

Because spirit moves outside of and unhindered by our orientation of time, we can now break habits sunk in time and undo destructive patterns that only yesterday seemed intractable. We are energy beings who temporarily live in a physical body; at deeper levels we know intuitively that much of this healing can take place at the energetic level without prolonged emotional catharsis.

In small ways: when you feel your true intent in a meeting or encounter has not come through, you can seek the assistance of your sacred partner to make things right. Simply share what has happened and how you feel about the encounter. If you have responsibility for what has happened, acknowledge this out loud. Then, discuss your genuine intention in that moment, what you wanted to happen and why. Ask spirit to insert your intention into the circumstance so that others might understand what you meant and why you did what you did. While this action requires honesty and humility on your part, spirit can then go "back" and clean things up and reduce much of the emotional damage that might have been triggered. You will notice a surprising ease when meeting this person or group next time.

In larger ways, whole regions of your life that have been emotionally charged can be entrusted to spirit. Simply request that the energetic charge dissipate and be replaced with greater clarity and peace. Emotions are energy with labels attached that we ourselves have made up. As you have learned in interim places, drop the labels (they're too confining and mostly illusion anyway) and focus on the energy that lies underneath.

I have had large amounts of rage, unforgiveness, anxiety and fear removed by doing nothing more than lying down, getting quiet, acknowledging my emotional state and seeking assistance from spirit to clear the energy block within me. When I need to return for another clearing I do. If your intent is to see things more clearly and for others to see you more clearly, this is best accomplished when emotional energy is acknowledged and then dissipated. Experiment with this yourself.

## ☽ *The Sacred Self observes*

*So much of what is required today involves unlearning your past. Unlearning and letting go of old beliefs, old definitions and old ways of behaving. Much of this is held in place by emotional energy. You feel good when you act in certain ways, while another action, even though it may prove to be healthier and more successful, feels threatening. Going back to discover why you are what you are may not always be necessary. A more elegant way is to move energetically and receive the release you desire. Keep the wisdom gained from earlier times but lose the emotional attachment. You have the power now to accomplish this. Earth life can be very challenging and you feel a wide range of emotions as you move through your days. This is good and very normal! When you discover patterns of unwanted feeling states washing over you and staying for long periods of time, however, this is another matter. Seek release, as this is not your inheritance and there are ways through.*

*We wish to say here that there is a place for medicine and for making sure you are not fighting your own body as you move through your days. Prolonged periods of anxiety, anger, fear and depression may reveal a biochemical lack of necessary nutrients. Do not fight your biology! Let go of the old definitions of what is good and bad and get the help you need through medicine and be on your way. There is no judgment here. You are loved and valued as you are.*

*Do not punish yourself with harsh judgment as you find old wounds that continue to show up. In time, you will see them as gifts given to you to remind you to turn to your spirit helpers. Maturity on this path is not measured by the absence of conflict, but in the time it takes you to recognize and surrender. Intend only that you might grow in your capacity to see things clearly a little more each day.*

## ☽ Success

Our culture values endless movement and activity and a continually ascending path towards the top. Little value is placed on internal shifts of the kind we speak of here. Interim places teach a key lesson that seems central to living in partnership with the sacred self: internal shifts in consciousness precede external changes in reality. What happens inside affects what will happen outside. Nothing changes until we do; everything eventually shifts only when we do. This is how things work.

I no longer need success in work in order to feel good. I know I keep repeating myself but I feel surprised and shocked when I say these words out loud! Did I actually write these words?

Let me breathe deeply and write that again. I no longer need success in work in order to feel good, to feel like a man, to feel like a contributing person on this beautiful planet. I enjoy much of my work and have fun with colleagues and clients, as I also continue finding ways to financially keep things afloat. I feel grateful that I have been able to do these things for many years. I no longer need, however, to work as a means to feel good about who I am. This feeling now generates from within. Your path, too, has been a journey from the external and superficial to the internal, subterranean curves and channels of the heart.

At this point in the journey through interim places, you come to recognize that *authentic, sacred success has everything to do with the following:*

➤ becoming whole and complete

➤ becoming a full partner with your sacred self

➤ being clear about who you are and about what really matters

➤ finding ways to bring all of what matters to fruition

➤ moving quickly and elegantly with your sacred self, whether this movement means being active or being still

➤ learning how to be peaceful in all circumstances

➤ returning to peacefulness when feeling stress

➤ knowing, at a deep level, you are safe, regardless of what appears to be happening around you

➤ teaching your children and others how to move in alignment with their own inner knowing

➤ supporting and encouraging others to dream and do with their lives what they came here to do and to be

➤ living with a full and open heart which is, in practice, not nearly as lofty as it sounds!

➤ seeing yourself as one member, no greater or less than others, of a community of beings, both human and other than human, who move together through this earthly experience. Knowing this causes you to act and move with greater reverence and respect for all things.

What could be more important? At the beginning of your ordeal in interim places you may have lost your light and much more. You traveled through dark places and spent nights in anguish. Now your light returns to you and you desire to contribute in ways that matter to you, first, and then to others. As you hold the light of this intention and remember who you are, there is movement, whether you do anything or nothing. You enter into a new relationship with your own life in which you enjoy each day more than ever and find as much joy and meaning in quiet days of solitude as you do when working with customers and colleagues. This shift restores life in you, vitality and playfulness.

## ❯ *The Sacred Self observes*

*We wish to add to your learnings about success these simple comments: Success involves learning how to see things more clearly. Your days in interim places have centered around learning how to see and let go of illusions about*

*tomorrow and yesterday and enter this moment as fully as you can. This is the simplicity on the other side of the fear that so easily besets you and many others. There is nothing you need hold and face alone, nothing you need hide and run from, for fear you will be shamed. There is no separation between you and us, or between you and others in your life. Others want and yearn for the same things as you do, even though their momentary appearance may tell a different story.*

*Very few of the existing structures in your culture encourage people to experience themselves and speak authentically with themselves and others. Workplaces, meetings and conferences, family gatherings, religious institutions, educational life at all levels all fail to call forth what is extraordinary and magnificent in humans. When others irritate you, know that you only see a part of the whole. You do not see essence . . . unless you look for it.*

*See things clearly. This is the most direct definition of success we see in you, dearest brother, yet think of the ground you have covered in order to arrive here!*

## ☽ *Solitude and balance*

I live at least two lives: a public life with clients, seminar participants and colleagues and a private, more introverted life with just myself, my internal company, my family and books. All of us have a public and a private life. In between these two worlds is a third world of reentry which surrounds either world. Reentry is a world we pass through when leaving one world for the other. It takes us anywhere from a minute to an hour or two or longer to pass through it. We need the time for reentry, even though we may not enjoy the experience of it; we can feel agitated, abrupt, impatient with everyone and with ourselves. It passes.

There is considerable fear about solitude. The vast majority of adults talk of the need to find more balance, yet they seldom pursue it. When you slow down the first feelings you experience are often not pleasant, and so many of us do not slow down at all. We fear the feelings of reentry will go on forever. Even when we do slow down, we fill our space with noise and distraction, as if there is something terrifying about simply being alone with ourselves. Interim places are times of unbidden solitude and you have learned that *solitude is terrifying!* The thoughts and feelings that wash over you are upsetting! But they pass. This is just reentry. I know now that I seriously underestimated my need for solitude and time for myself earlier in my life. I do not want to make that mistake again.

All of the pressures we feel are external pressures: do more for our family, do more for our work, do more activities with our friends. There are no cultural pressures to withdraw in solitude. You only have the distress signals from the body which you have begun to listen to more than ever: the stiff necks and tight shoulders, the headaches and sore feet. The body does not lie. It does not know how to.

When you have been forced into solitude and found that you can thrive there, you will not be easily tempted again by the seductive promises that endless activity and busyness bring.

You will instead enjoy your solitude and drink it in, like spring plants drink in light from the sun and water from the earth. You will begin to see, as I have, that your relationship with solitude is just as organic and basic to your life as sunlight and water. Extroverts require solitude to deepen and balance decisions and direction; introverts need time alone to replenish and restore their energy. Solitude is an important doorway into the sacred for all of us. It was in solitude, after all, that you made contact with sacred guidance, with the sacred self, with the possibility of a partnership both with others and with God.

It is in solitude (after interaction with others) that your best work is conceived and then given form. It is in solitude that you rest and nourish yourself after working in the world. Sometimes you share solitude with intimate others, sometimes you spend it alone. It is a time to be with yourself, rather than a time to do things. You may have to negotiate with others for this time, and the negotiation may require courage and patience. Entrust this intention to your partners and move forward. As you allow time to simply be, much gets done.

## ❯ *The Sacred Self observes*

*To be alone with your self is a great and beautiful gift. So many people fear this and actually arm themselves against its possibility through endless activity and busyness. Yet as you, our partner, correctly say, the surprise that comes to you when you are alone with your self is that you are not alone. You are present with another, your (higher or sacred) self (or soul, spirit, life force) with whom all things in life can be created. Are you afraid you will find nothing if you look? Do not remain afraid but take your fear into your solitude and allow it to slip away. Lay it aside as you might a sweater you no longer need and let your self reveal itself (your essence) to you. We do not speak here about doctrine but about knowing with assurance that you are not alone, that you have assistance, loving power and hope available to you and in you.*

*When you leave your solitude for work in the world, you can leave in a grounded, secure place, knowing that you have an inner home where you may return. Because of this place within, all activity in the outside world can be lighter, done with greater ease and more joy. Even when you lose your temper or feel frustrated with your day, you need not stay in this place for long. There is help within.*

*Your culture paints a picture of solitude as a place where selfishness prevails, but this image is inaccurate. When you go into the world without being grounded in who you are, you will exhaust yourself and not serve the world's needs. The opposite dynamic is also fraught with difficulty: when you spend all of your time alone with no connection to your world, you will make yourself brittle and dry. The resulting narcissism and selfishness both describe a stance of being ungrounded in the true self and trying unsuccessfully to find compensatory satisfaction in the world. Many suffer from keeping all distorted self images and fears to themselves, while seldom allowing the light of truth from others in the world. The resulting self-absorption allows them neither to influence others nor to be influenced by others.*

*A correct balance between the self and the world is required. In your culture, the adjustments often need to be made in your relationship to solitude. Open yourself to it. Find your self in it. Learn to rest, play and relax, letting go even of your need to learn and grow. These will happen. For now, the task is joy!*

## ❯ Time

Mid-life carries with it an increased sense of urgency in me. I feel aware of the shortness of life and its fragility as well. I do not want to waste my time here. Interim places have carved a deep but loving space in me with the same subtlety with which a summer breeze alters the current of a river. I feel changed now but do not know exactly how or when this happened. I know that what is mine will come to me; I do not have to force action, or to worry and fret over missed opportunities. I take what action I can to move toward the outcomes I want. I allow things to run their course because I know things are seldom what they seem. My sense of urgency has been replaced with a sense of vigilance and curiosity.

Our lives can change with one phone call or with a single, unforeseen encounter. All the plans, dreams and hopes can be realized or vanquished in an instant. We each know this in our body. In the past, we attempted to control many things in our lives because we feared everything would all fall apart if we did not. It fell apart anyway! We have learned that, in crisis, we experience time wrapped and bound in the illusion of separation from spirit, that things are far away in time and space. When we realize that we are one with all things and connected with all that matters to us, we begin to shift our stance regarding time. Time begins to lose its grasp on us. Ironically, we then begin to see our moments, days and lives more seriously and more fragile. Stripped of the urgency of time, we hold our days as precious gifts to enjoy.

One day while walking at the reservoir, I smelled smoke from a distant fire. Men worked on a tar roof a half mile away. Then I felt this nudge.

## ☽ *The Sacred Self observes*

*This is how it is with fulfillment of your intention. It is not far away from you but it is present in you now, fully accomplished. Desire and its fulfillment are of one and the same energy; they balance each other and always come as one energy. Like the smoke, they are in you now, even though you thought completion was far away in time and distance. What you see and have always seen as far away is within you.*

*There is no time. There is no distance or separation between what you intend (in your open heart) and the ful-fillment of this intention. When you are able to see and hold them as one unified energy, you will be able to create what you want and sustain it more consistently. This is the new land you are moving into and will write about in the future.*

I knew at once this information felt right but was imme-diately frustrated that it took me so much time to "get it." I also knew that trying hard to "get it" would only agitate me more; wisdom is revealed to an open heart in its time, not always during the time we have allotted on our calen-dar. We want everything good to happen now and every-thing painful to be delayed until much later, thank you. The universe delivers what we need at the right time, in the right circumstances with the right people. To the open heart, there are no missed opportunities. What is ours comes to us.

We are each asked to let go of old ways and open to new ways of being. Managers who have been fired no longer manage, and must learn who they want to be now. Sales people who no longer sell, engineers who have been laid off as engineers, parents whose children are gone now, men who are no longer able to do and be the men our culture once valued, women who move into leadership, must all die to old ways of being and adopt to whole new behavior sets. The signs are there: this is a time of inner death and rebirth. A time of shifting our consciousness in order to move more easily in the new millennium. As you read these words in your solitude today, they mark the movement you have experienced in interim places.

When part of us dies, it feels like we are wasting time and going nowhere. Depression and grieving are common. Anger and bitterness are typical ways we disguise the deeper sadness we actually feel. Our value and self-esteem are at all-time lows, since both are measured against straight advancement through time in the external world. Interim places trick our notion of time, even as winter tricks us into believing everything green has died. In truth, everything is restored anew, shifted and changed, and put back together again.

It is the putting back together again that requires faith in interim places. It may feel like there cannot possibly be time enough for this to happen. There may not be. But your concept of time itself (wrapped tightly with success, advancement and managing how you appear to significant others) has been one of the important items that is dying now in you, along with its sharp edge of comparison and approval. Your work is to honor its passing.

You may have noticed that you have a sense of peace in this place now, a sense that your life has unfolded just as it needed to, for reasons that are more clear now than before. Your relationships with others have taken on a new depth and clarity, while many others are still struggling to make sense out of the turmoil that seems to steal much of who they mistook themselves to be. Standing faithfully as your life does what it needs to do prepares you for the unique service you offer to others in your life who value and want the quiet confidence that is now yours.

## ❯ *The Sacred Self observes*

*Your culture's view of time has both served you and robbed you of a vital connection with the spirit dimension. Much good has come from the sense of urgency and the pace with which you are able to move and assemble yourselves and get great things done. When the time comes for things to die and realign, yes even transfigure into new ways of being and working, this same sense of urgency can become your* enemy. *Is it surprising that so many who undergo radical medical procedures report a common learning afterwards: their sense of time has been altered and what they do with their time often changes.*

*Much of the trouble with your view of time is that it is wrapped tightly with your images of the future which are treated as if they are real and fixed. As our partner has written about earlier, the antidote to living with images and fears of the future is to settle into the life that is yours to live today. Today is the only place where the spiritual power of partnership can be released. How could it be otherwise? So live the life that is in you to live today. Look for small things to give thanks for, beginning with the earth you walk or ride on today. Open yourself to the knowing place within that always says one thing: I am with you, you are not alone here.*

## ❯ *Abundance and security*

One year before the events of this book began, I read a marvelous book by Marlo Morgan called *Mutant Message Down Under.*[2] I read it as a true account of an American woman who takes an "unplanned" trip into the Australian outback with a tribe of aborigines who claim they heard her cry for assistance. She travels with them for many months as they walk across the country. This tribe possesses almost nothing yet live with a daily provision of all they require. Food, water, clothing and cure all become available when they are needed. I wept at the simplicity and power with which they lived.

They had everything I yearned for: complete harmony and interdependence with the universe. Was this why I cried as I read?

The tribe celebrated each morning in advance of the provision they knew would come their way later in the day.

They sang songs of gratitude to the earth and to its plant and animal life that would present themselves to the tribe for healing and nourishment. I felt captivated not by their faith but by their absolute knowing that all would be perfect. *A single, simple tune.*

It seems fitting that as my interim place began with fears of scarcity and lack, I should end with reflections on abundance. Many months after reading Morgan's book I would find myself in my own "outback" experience. My newfound guides gently reminded me that they had come in response to the cry of an open heart. I knew then, as now, that I co-create everything that happens in my life. Sometimes I know why and sometimes not. All of the struggle in these pages has been about finding my way back into harmony with self and the universe. My struggle, and yours too, has been about learning to live fullheartedly with the inner knowing that all is perfect.

Our western mind tells us that abundance has to do with how much material and financial wealth we have stored and held in reserve. Our security is tied directly to how high and wide the stockpile is. Interim places reveal many different kinds of abundance even as there are many kinds of intelligence. There is abundance of finance, abundance of health and abundance of peace and joy. Abundance also applies to intimacy and authenticity in relationships, to creative ideas, to an abiding sense of purpose, meaning and destiny. When we see the whole picture more clearly, we are abundant in many ways. Our vision becomes clearer in these interim places.

I sat down recently to prepare for two days of retreat work with a health care management group. I did not feel anything was coming to me as I worked so I did other things. I did not worry because I knew my process; I knew the agenda and design for this conference would become clear to me when needed. The night before I was to leave, the entire design for the two days dropped into my mind in two or three seconds. Virtually complete. I wrote down what had come to me. More came as I began to work with the team. The two days went beautifully. This, the guides say, is the new abundance.

## ❯ *The Sacred Self observes*

*The new abundance is having all you need when you need it. It has to do with being continually resourced through your relationship with spirit and with your sacred self. It includes daily sustenance of all things from tangible, material goods to states of internal feeling. Abundance springs forth from relationship. You experience this continual resourcing, dearest one, even as you write these words and near the completion of this project. You and all who read these words have the capacity to experience this abundance. It is your birthright, waiting to be claimed. Do so in love, knowing these things are given in great love for you and for all who join you in the journey of union with the sacred self.*

## ❯ *Tools for the Journey*

### How to walk in the new partnership with spirit and your sacred self:

➤ Give your spoken intention for this partnership in order for it to continue being made more real, visible and active in your life.

➤ Find a way to create a sacred ritual to celebrate your decision for partnership. Acknowledge all of the events that brought you to this moment, speak of what you've learned and what you've struggled with. Turn and face this moment and call in the assistance, comfort and companionship that you need from your sacred partners.

➤ Pay special attention to times when you're upset and feeling a need to do something. Ask, "Does this serve my fear or my essence?" Then decide what to do.

➤ Gratitude, balancing activity with solitude, doing things that bring you joy. You know the routine by now.

➤ Surrender. Each day invite spirit in to all aspects of your life and into the lives of those with whom you share important connection. Continue watching and recording what happens. And enjoy your wild life.

# The Warrior

The warriors tame
The beasts in their past
So that the night's hoofs
Can no longer break the jeweled vision
In the heart.
The intelligent and the brave
Open every closet in the future and evict
All the mind's ghosts who have the bad habit
Of barfing everywhere.
For a long time the universe
Has been germinating in your spine
But only a saint has the talent,
The courage to slay
The past giant, the future anxieties.
The warrior
Wisely sits in a circle with others
Gathering the strength to unmask Himself,
Then
Sits, giving
Like a great illumined planet on
The
Earth

—Hafiz[1]

### CHAPTER 12

## Standing in the Fire Without Getting Burned
Notes for those who would help

THIS chapter is for leaders who may be called upon to help those in crisis. It is divided into two segments. One is for leaders in organizations who need to pay attention to signs that some of the people who work with them may be suffering grief and trauma from any number of downsizings, mergers and other organizational restructurings that have claimed the careers of colleagues. Also, employees who have survived divorce, death of loved ones and other crises outlined in this book bring these dilemmas into the organization each day. We cannot simply shut down aspects of life that are troubling us (even though we try to and often think we succeed). The second is for leaders at home who must somehow care for loved ones who are suffering. For both sets of leaders the questions are similar: What kind of help is helpful and what help is no help at all?

Hafiz says to us that leaders tame the past and future in order that the "jeweled vision of the heart" may not be broken. As war with Iraq continued when I wrote this chapter I felt that Hafiz' notion of what it meant to be a warrior was quite different than the images I saw on CNN. Above all, leaders today are called to be guardians of the "jeweled vision of the heart" of people. What does this mean? For me and other leaders with whom I have been graced to live and work over the years, I suggest it means we lose our regrets or cautions from the past and our careful, self-saving strategies for the future. Only then can we pay attention to matters of the heart and make these matters part of the bottom line we claim to serve today.

# ❯ *Notes for leaders in the workplace*

Out of the heart proceeds vision and commitment, a yearning, to do something important, to contribute something that matters through our lives and work. Out of the heart proceeds truth, a willingness to engage authentically with others, to care deeply about one another and commit ourselves to quality relationships and workmanship in what we do. Our heart yields all variation of feelings, desires, doubts and fears. The spirit of a place, of a team or organization, is held in the heart of its people. Breakthroughs in productivity and innovation, turning points in a team's progress and alignment are found or lost depending on the quality of heart engagement. For leaders who miss these issues, you will miss many other things as well. For leaders who find the "jeweled vision of the heart," you have found everything.

This book is about another more troubling aspect of the heart's vision: the heart at times leads us into interim places where everything we have seen, treasured and valued is lost. The best we can do is stand and watch our lives do what they will do. All understanding and control are lost. You have people working with you for whom this experience is a current reality. This experience is as natural as the rain in the north and heat in the south. It often portends a significant realigning of the self, a new orientation to life and work, and may give rise to new jeweled vision of the heart. Nobody knows. Your first and essential message to others is: *"This is a normal occurrence. You're not crazy."*

I have argued these times are precious beyond measure and must be held as sacred. Above all, people who are in the throes of interim places feel vulnerable, often terrified, overwhelmed and inadequate in ways that defy description. They need to be nurtured and supported. Here are a handful of proven guidelines to help you with colleagues at work who may be struggling with issues discussed in this book.

## ❯ *Above all else, work on yourself.*

The culture at work is a reflection of the consciousness of leaders at all levels. It's not a dynamic that exists out there or with those above us. It's in us and proceeds from us! We are each carriers. This means that our individual actions as leaders matter. Hafiz asks that, as warriors, we *learn to let go of the beasts of the past and mind's ghosts of the future.* What does this mean? More importantly, how does this letting go enable leaders to do warrior's work?

The cultures in our workplaces often contain a healthy dose of the "never let them see you sweat" mind set. Any hint of vulnerability is taboo and even the slightest indication of neediness is considered a direct threat to one's career. Failure is avoided at all costs. These dynamics are true for white men (like the author) in organizations and even more true for white women, men and women of color, and gay, lesbian, and bisexual people of all races. Simply put: emotional vulnerability is seen as "not good." Pay close attention to your experience today. Be mindful of what drives your behavior. What do you do with your own fears and concerns, your own need to learn? How do you play out the culture in which you operate? What is your contribution?

First, recognize the box for what it is: a reality we have had a hand in creating. There is no research that supports the notion that high productivity proceeds from such a stance (just the opposite). Pay attention to your own tendency to:

1. Take on more and more work and set impossible deadlines as an effort to prove yourself and your worth to some mythical boss somewhere. This alleged path to safety is not safe (many good people are laid off) and creates considerable hardship for colleagues around you. Learn how to set limits and say no while offering options to those above you; this is a key developmental step for all leaders. Take it. Remember, if everything with you is negotiable it means that nothing is truly valuable to you. You can cause considerable damage while believing you're doing great work.

   Letting go of future concerns about how you will be seen is one of the ghosts Hafiz speaks of. The challenge is to invest fully in the day you are in, without undue concerns about what has happened in the past or what might happen tomorrow. Make sure that when you say "Yes" to assignments, your "Yes" is responsive to the legitimate demands of the organization and not simply because you are afraid to say "No."

2. Cover up and dismiss the emotional needs of others because you've never acknowledged your own fears and concerns. Perhaps you've been busy trying to win the approval of important others above you, by fitting in and appeasing them and not authentically putting yourself on the map by expressing what you really think and feel. This is a common but flawed strategy of preserving your place at the organizational table.

   The trouble is this strategy costs you your own humanity. The cost to your colleagues is there may be no leader who steps up and speaks to the emotional trauma people may be experiencing. Undertake to begin building a culture in and around your team that allows for authentic expression of feeling; doing only this will help you build an organization that you'd be proud to have your loved ones work in. Isn't this a good litmus test for your effectiveness as a leader?

## ❭ *Secret openings, hidden doorways: how to know when people may be hurting.*

Pay attention to people who suddenly become quieter, more remote. Watch for sudden and unexplained increases or decreases in time spent at work. Listen for changes in the style or tone of others' communication and shifts in the quality of work. Pay attention to expressions of bitterness and anger that seem disproportionate to what has taken place. Listen carefully to the space between words, a shallow breathing, a voice that comes only from the throat and not the whole body. Look for eyes that refuse to meet your own, in ways that feel different to you. These can be signs of fear or exhaustion from carrying a heavy weight for an extended period of time.

## ❭ *Tools for the Journey*

**How leaders can help. Pay attention to the present.**

➤ There is much you do not see and cannot know without compassionate inquiry.

➤ People at work often keep their feelings hidden as a way to insure they are seen as "good team players."

Trauma kept to oneself can leave people suffering in a strange and damaging silence that unfortunately characterizes many corporate cultures today. The best strategy is to pay attention and be willing to slow down for a period of time so you will be able to move more quickly later. Continuing to force the action and keep driving results now may well bring your unit to a grinding halt later.

➤ **Engage people where they are before demanding they move.**

➤ Invite people to share how they are doing when you know they have been through tough times. Don't assume that because the corporate transition appears to be going well from your lofty vantage point in the hierarchy that others below you are having a similar experience. Nothing could be further from the truth.

➤ Find ways to check in with individuals and with teams you feel may be struggling with their own or organizational dilemmas. Do this more than you feel it necessary and continue doing it longer than you have in the past. Future performance depends on it. Why not use the uncertainty of the present to consciously create a more compassionate culture where the jeweled treasure people bring with them each day is genuinely treasured. Watch what happens to your innovation, climate, service delivery and quality when people realize they don't have to leave heart issues and other vital aspects of themselves out in the employee parking lot.

Remember, make room for all the house guests!

The organizational research literature is replete with case examples of what happens when change efforts are forced down the throats of employees, who are advised to simply suck up their grief and uncertainty and keep moving. David Noer, in particular, argues for a focused campaign to ensure the hearts and minds of people are brought along in the aftermath of significant corporate upheaval. In his classic book, *Healing the Wounds: Overcoming the Trauma of Layoffs and Revitalizing Downsized Organizations*, Noer states a compelling case for creating meeting structures that allow people to speak of their loss, the fear associated with drastic change, as well as their hope for the future. Though most cultures fail to encourage full expression of feeling, those which do realize significant gains in espirit de corp, trust and readiness to move forward with greater resiliency, responsiveness and courage.

Sometimes these interventions can be simple and fairly quick, other times a more extensive intervention needs to be crafted. Nothing in the way of renewed productivity will be gained until people are allowed space to share their emotional state. Like a strategic time out in a sports event, when leaders create space for emotional time outs, the organization can once again move quickly into the future because it has first slowed down to engage people where they are.

Slow down to go quicker. People who suffer, when met in the place of suffering, are much more willing to go with you where you want to go. But, none of us are talked out of our grief and loss when a leader's words and actions imply we're weak, self-absorbed, disloyal or uncommitted if our feelings don't immediately lift. I am citing specific cases from my consulting practice where people were essentially told these things by their managers! There must be a better way.

# ❭ *Words and action that meet others where they are:*

➤ "Tell me how you are doing . . ."

➤ " I wanted to check in with you . . ."

➤ " I know I'd be feeling frightened and a bit lost if something like this happened to me...how are you doing?"

➤ "If it's OK with you, I will not wait for you to ask for what you might be needing. I will check in with you myself...you're important to me and to this team..."

➤ "Take some time and check in with our Employee Assistance people. It's confidential. I used them myself last year for several months and found it invaluable . . ."

➤ "I had a similar setback a few years back and felt very hurt and wounded by what happened. For awhile I felt lost and didn't know what to do. Are you in a similar place?"

Each of these statements is an opening presented to your colleague. Each requires courage and compassion, and obligates you then to listen to and accept what is shared with you in return. Mostly, they require you to simply be present, to allow your being to be enough with or without the right words. Our culture reacts with a bizarre combination of fascination and fear toward death and suffering; we want to look from a distance and then have it all go away before the first commercial. Your colleagues' plight may not disappear as quickly or as beautifully as you wish, but your presence and compassion will greatly help.

# ❯ *Release your concerns to your higher power.*

Make it a point to pray for, call in help for, invoke assistance toward, send positive energy to those people and circumstances at work you're concerned about. This stance does not mean you are weak, but wise; practical spirituality begins with allowing spirit to work in the daily challenges of your life. Pay attention to what happens.

The basic premise of this book is that challenging times open an unusual doorway to the sacred that, as we walk through, can equip us with new awareness and resources. Apply the same principles to others who you care about. Test this for yourself in the real world of your work life.

# ❯ *Notes for leaders at home*

In her book, *The Invitation,* Oriah Mountain Dreamer challenges each of us with these invitations to live more fully and courageously:

> *It doesn't interest me what planets are squaring your moon. I want to know if you have touched the center of your own sorrow, if you have been opened by life's betrayals or have become shriveled and closed from fear of further pain. I want to know if you can sit with pain, mine or your own, without moving to hide it or fade it or fix it. I want to know if you can see beauty even when it's not pretty and if you can source your life from ITS presence. It doesn't interest me who you are or how you came to be here. I want to know if*

*you will stand in the center of the fire with*
*me and not shrink back.*[2]

Our work as helpers is not to do things for others but to
be things for others. Our challenge is not to demand that
others change but, by managing our own feelings and reactions, to be with them in a way that is different. Oriah
Mountain Dreamer again confirms what we have seen earlier in this book, that when circumstances in our life (i.e., the
behavior of those we care about) are troubling or, worse,
destructive, our best way of helping is by managing ourselves and our reactions. Here are some guidelines that may
help.

## ❯ Tools for the Journey
## How you can help those at home

### Ask: "Whose problem is it?"

Even when someone's behavior is troubling to you it
remains their problem to resolve. When it becomes your
problem and you're working to resolve it, then you're in
the way! Your help is no longer helpful. Establish or
tighten up the boundaries that distinguish your life from
others. What is OK with you and what is not OK? What
consequences can you set up for when others violate your
boundaries? If you commit yourself to developing clarity
around your own boundaries you will often feel guilty
and selfish in the early stages. These are indicators of
health and invitations for you to continue! People need to
find their own way through transitions. Part of our work
is to stay out of the way while at the same time offering
support and the wisdom of our own experience with similar times.

### Release with love those you care about.

Surrender or release those people and circumstances you care about to your higher power, in whatever way you understand this term. This essential decision requires a commitment to let the other person go, day by day, and to gradually stop attempting to control what happens to him/her. This is very difficult work and requires the assistance of your spirit guidance as well. For most of us, this is not a transcendent moment replete with lights and bells and descending angels singing hymns in the sky. It is an act of desperation taken only after everything else we've tried to do has failed.

### Surrender quickly, consistently and often.

Invite your spirit guidance to assist with both external circumstances and internal feeling states (i.e., anger, rage, fear, despair). Your internal feeling state is a good barometer of how hard you continue to grasp the situation to make something happen. Consider the possibility that you need and are able to make nothing happen, on your own. Take action only on those matters that you deem controllable by you; release what cannot be controlled to your spirit guidance. Ask for discernment so that over time you can see the difference.

### Notice how controlling you are even when surrendering!

It is good to know what you want and it is generally healthy to be clear about your intentions. Yet we're looking at times in life that are mysterious and full of uncertainty. Rather than spend countless hours assessing whether a development is good or bad, helpful or a hindrance, I have found it useful to simply state:

*"I want what is highest and best for all concerned, even though I don't know what this means or what it looks like."*
Having released circumstances and people with this intention, I am thereby freed to do the most important thing I can do: live my life as fully as possible *even though circumstances are unresolved.* To delay my own life until things are resolved with someone else's life makes my contentment, serenity and enjoyment dependent upon something outside of my direct control. I have lived like this in the past and it was not healthy. Interim places taught me a better way to live that I pass on to you: *live now!*

**Find ways to take care of yourself.**

You are of little help to others if you're exhausted or wracked with bitterness or jealousy. Starting with small things, find ways to nurture, replenish and restore yourself. Going to movies in the afternoon is one way that I do this. Buying small treats is another. Taking a walk through the park instead of driving is another. Unresolved challenges invite us to find new ways of being in relationship with them and with ourselves. Frequent "time outs" is one ingredient. While you cannot know what will happen to the one you love, you can and must resolve that you will come out of this time stronger, healthier, more resilient and whole. Every time you treat yourself with kindness remind yourself this is part of the plan.

**Cultivate a stance of gratefulness.**

The most radical aspect of this new partnership with the sacred can be the most difficult. I have learned it, forgotten it and relearned it many times. Under stress it can be the first thing I forget. When I turn the corner in difficult situations it is often only after I return to gratefulness. The stance of gratefulness essentially means that we welcome all experiences into our life as house guests. The good and the bad, just and unjust, right and wrong. We receive them as if our spirit partners stood in front of us and hand delivered them to us with the invitation to "Take and enjoy! This is made especially for you!"

Gratefulness delivers us, benefits us, frees us, and lightens us to enjoy the life we are given today without the need to continually assess, compare, ask "Why?" or judge. Gratefulness allows us to notice all the small wonders present each day that bring to our lives beauty, grace and a sense of belonging. The rainbow that appears right there in your back yard after a summer rain. The sparrows busy bathing in the driveway puddle. The statements made in the meeting that show subtle but real shifts in a good direction. The unexpected phone call from child to simply ask, "How are you doing?" Gratefulness allows us to see what we would otherwise miss if we were frustrated and fighting with our own life.

The difficult passages of interim places require from each of us a certain faithfulness and courage to live more and more present each day. Present to ourselves and others. When I'm in the presence of someone who is mentally, emotionally, spiritually present and available to me that is usually enough! They don't have to do anything! Words are not always needed. Sometimes your presence itself and the relationship with another is enough to sustain a person through the dark night. Commit to being present and witness the courage, persistence and resiliency required by this part of the path through interim places. Let this be enough.

## ❯ *The Sacred Self observes*

*Our time with you, dearest one, and with those who read this book is drawing to an end. You rest in a serenity that once eluded you, you enjoy the blessings of home, love, work and health you once feared were lost forever. You ask now how others can best intervene with and help those who experience tough times and great uncertainty. We say to you that partnership between people and their spirit guidance (in whatever form this takes for each person) is a gift to be totally used up by you! Do not settle for small, pre-packaged boxes of what others tell you this must look, sound and feel like, for each of you is wondrously unique. You each have been given your own way of connecting with your spirit guidance. Find your own way into this partnership today and familiarize yourself with the ways in which you and spirit move and dance; only then will you be able to see and appreciate the movement of spirit in another's life.*

*When trouble arises, look within (at your beliefs, feelings and assumptions) and find why it feels like trouble to you. What fears have been evoked and why are they seen as fears at all? And then, release all to spirit but remain vigilant. Look within, look beyond. This is the key. Know that there is much you may not see in the life of another and that, even though their momentary suffering may be hard for them and you, rest in knowing that as you look within, and then beyond, that you will accomplish much. You do damage only when you fail to look within and instead grasp and force action without first looking beyond for assistance. Utilize all the resources available to you and do not let your beliefs about what is "out there" stand in your way. Life is too special, too extraordinary to be undone by small opinions that are held as truth. Let go of anything that stops you from enjoying the beauty, peace and fullness that is yours. It will go well with you then. Be in peace with yourself and others and know you are prized beyond measure.*

It rains here in Connecticut today. A warm, summer wind blows and rattles the windows nearby. I have only wanted to celebrate the deep spiritual union I have known since I came into this life, a relationship which emerged stronger in interim places. We are not alone here nor left to our own devices, even though it feels this way at times. My work is to remind you of the truth that is in you. Your work is to receive all that is yours, from these pages, and leave the rest. It is for someone else. Take what is yours and use it to bring love into your world today in small, unseen ways. Be faithful to the moment you are in and know with certainty that having done this, everything else will work out for you. It has for me.

*May the energy in these words be a blessing to you.*

## Nothing is Wasted

*I once met the old man I will become*
*but only for an instant*
*where a decision to love or hold back*
*needed to be faced.*
*"What will you say to me when*
*we meet again?" he asked.*
*"I lived fully," I replied, and with that*
*he disappeared.*
*Strange, you say, that our future lives in us now?*
*I once met the African chief I had been*
*in another time when everything I loved*
*had been lost. Nothing was recovered,*
*not even me.*
*"What will you ask of me?" I wondered.*
*"Heal my wounded heart," he said,*
*"that I might fly again*
*and be on my way."*
*The timing was perfect, I knew what to do.*

*I took the grief anchor into me,*
*wept bitterly for a time and released it to*
*the Great Spirit*
*so that the chief, buoyant with gratitude,*
*became a wind guide, the unseen leader,*
*silent healer and supplier from the secret place*
*of the Most High.*
*Strange, you say, that our past lives in us now?*
*Listen: we are each a great treasure.*
*Every suffering and every joy adds to our luminance.*
*Nothing is wasted here.*
*The exuberant cry of achievement*
*the lonely howling in the middle of the night*
*the tears of gratitude that suddenly appear*
*and slide down the cheeks*
*like a creek in spring*
*all add to the great beauty*
*that is me.*
*And what about you?*

—D.H.[3]

# APPENDIX A

## NOTES
Attributions for chapter poetry and prose quotations.
Publication data for note entries are in the Bibliography.

### PREFACE
1. Rumi, Jelalu'l-Din (1207–1273). "Guest House."
   From *The Essential Rumi*. Coleman Barks, John
   Moyne trans. Harper, San Francisco, 1995.

### CHAPTER 1
1. Holden, Daniel. "Waking Up." Unpublished poem,
   1996.

### CHAPTER 2
1. Holden, Daniel. "Saving Yourself." Unpublished
   poem, 1998.

### CHAPTER 3
1. Chuang-Tzu (369?–286? B.C.E.). "Cutting Up An
   Ox." Cited in *The Enlightened Heart*. Stephen
   Mitchell ed. Harper Perennial, 1989.
2. Rilke, Rainer Maria. "It's possible I am pushing
   through." From *Book of Hours*. 1905. Cited in
   *Selected Poems*. Robert Bly trans. HarperCollins,
   1981.

### CHAPTER 4
1. Rumi. "The Question." Original poem c 1207–1273.
   Cited in *Open Secret Versions of Rumi*. John
   Moyne and Coleman Barks trans. Threshold Books,
   1984.
2. Rilke, Rainer Maria. "It's possible I am pushing
   through." From *Book of Hours*. *ibid.*
3. *ibid*

CHAPTER 5
1. Hafiz. "It Has Not Rained Light." Original poem
   c 1320–1389. *ibid*
2. Rilke, Rainer Maria. "It's possible I am pushing
   through." From *Book of Hours, ibid.*

CHAPTER 6
1. Chodrön, Pema. *Start Where You Are: A Guide to
   Compassionate Living,* 1994.
2. Rilke, Rainer Maria. "A Man Watching." From
   *Book of Pictures.* 1902, 1906. Cited in *Selected
   Poems.* Robert Bly trans. HarperCollins, 1981.

CHAPTER 7
1. Holden, Daniel. "Constellation." Unpublished
   poem, 1997.
2. Rilke, Rainer Maria. "It's possible I am pushing
   through." *ibid*
3. *ibid*
4. Rumi, Jelalu'l-Din. "Say Yes Quickly." Original
   poem c 1207–1273. Cited in *Open Secret Versions
   of Rumi.* John Moyne and Coleman Barks trans.
   Threshold Books, 1984.
5. Rilke, Rainer Maria. "My life is not this steeply
   sloping hour." From *Book of Hours. ibid.*
6. Rumi, Jelalu'l-Din. "Say Yes Quickly." *ibid.*
7. Rilke, Rainer Maria. "It's possible I am pushing
   through." *ibid.*

CHAPTER 8
1. Stafford,William. "Reminders." From *Learning to
   Live in The World: Earth Poems.* Laura Apol and
   Jerry Watson ed. Harcourt, 1994.
2. Rilke, Rainer Maria. "A Man Watching." From
   *Book of Pictures. ibid*

3. *ibid*
4. Rilke, Rainer Maria. "Whoever grasps the contradictions." From *Book of Hours, ibid.*
5. Rilke, Rainer Maria. "The Swan." From *New Poems.* 1907, 1908. Cited in *Selected Poems.* Robert Bly trans. 1981.
6. Wordsworth, William. *William Wordsworth – the Major Works.* Stephen Gill ed. 1988.
7. Rilke, Rainer Maria. "It's possible I am pushing through." *ibid.*

CHAPTER 9
1. Jimenez, Juan Ramon. "Oceans." Cited in *News of the Universe: Poems of Twofold Consciousness.* Robert Bly ed. 1980.

CHAPTER 10
1. Blum, Ralph. *The Book of Runes.* 1993
2. Leggett, Travor. "The New Flute" (author unknown). *Zen and the Ways.* 1978.
3. Wordsworth, William. *William Wordsworth. ibid.*

CHAPTER 11
1. Stafford, William. "The Dream of Now." Cited in *Learning to Live in the World: Earth Poems. ibid*
2. Morgan, Marlo. *Mutant Message Down Under.* 1991.

CHAPTER 12
1. Hafiz. "The Warrior." Cited in *The Gift; Poems by Hafiz, The Great Sufi Master. ibid.*
2. Dreamer, Oriah Mountain. *The Invitation.* 1999.3. Holden, Daniel. "Nothing Wasted." 2003

APPENDIX  B

**TOOLS FOR THE JOURNEY**
Chapter summaries of what to do to continue moving
through your transformation.

CHAPTER 1
How to establish relationship with your sacred self:

➤ State your intention out loud, "I want to open a relationship with my sacred self, my essence."
➤ Open to the concerns and fears you might experience
and share these with your sacred self and with another person. If you come from a religious background you
might experience the sacred self as idolatry. Share this
and ask for direction.
➤ Ask for proof of this connection and then pay attention. Your proof will likely come very quickly and in
ways unique to you.
➤ Find a way of getting quiet for a few minutes and making contact on a regular basis. Speaking, writing, walking, sitting in nature are good places to start.
➤ Say yes quickly to small indicators that your life is out
of balance and that attention is needed in your heart.
Increases in stress, irritation, anger, small accidents
and injuries, coupled with feelings like you're having
to push too hard to make even small things turn in a
desired direction are indicators that you best stop and
reflect.
➤ Pay special attention to feelings of loneliness, sadness,
and a longing that is hard to describe to others.
Sometimes, as our spirit (sacred self) draws close, we
experience a hunger for connection.

CHAPTER 2
How to recognize you're entering interim places and a
time of transformation:

➤ Basic life systems are threatened. Your health, home,
family, core relationships, finances appear to be directly at risk.

➤ Current or anticipated sources of your supply dry up or
disappear altogether. Financial resources are lost; medical strategies and resources fail; a partner leaves and
does not come back.

➤ Your proven strategies for recovery no longer work for
you. Industriousness, effort, hard work and will power
no longer seem to matter at all but instead yield
greater degrees of frustration.

➤ Your capacity to remain present to the demands and
joys of each day slowly but unmistakingly erodes, giving way to the suffocating sandstorms of an imagined
and terrifying future. The loss of this capacity to simply be present is especially felt at night, or in other
quiet moments. Mental noise makes sleep difficult.
Frustration slowly gives way to fear and then despair.

➤ Momentary gains are washed out with further losses
and longer periods of unbidden solitude and uncertainty. Quick attempts to fix the situation, to right the
sinking ship of your life, fail to yield lasting results.
Things grow better then turn sharply worse.

➤ At some point fear becomes the predominant emotion
you feel each day as you grip your life tighter and
tighter, thinking your grasp will make you safe.

➤ Know with certainty that others have passed this way.
There is a way through. This time will pass.

CHAPTER 3
What to do in *No Light:*

➤ Trust your inner voice of the heart. It has night vision and works intuitively by knowing the next step you should take. In the absence of having a clear plan in your head, the intuitive wisdom of the heart often knows what to do, but only for right now. In this moment.

➤ Become quiet, inquire and wait.

➤ Watch for serendipitous signs, chance run-ins with colleagues and friends, TV and media events that seem to grab your attention. Celebrate when they occur; do not concern yourself when they don't.

➤ Assume you are in the right place at the right time. All that is yours will come to you.

➤ Be open to moving in ways that may feel new and different.

CHAPTER 4
What to do when you fear *All is Lost:*

➤ Allow yourself space and time for grieving what has been lost. Anger is often a surface feeling hiding a deeper experience of fear and sadness. See if you can feel these, and then release them to God, as you understand Him.

➤ Be especially gentle and compassionate with yourself; you are in a terrain that many others avoid at all cost, and so bring added suffering to themselves and their families.

➤ Watch out for the tendency to imagine the worst catastrophes happening in the future and then fearing them now, as if they are the only possibility. When I come to this place with my fear of what the situation looks like, my sacred self says, "So it seems," as if it knows what is truly going on. Example: My assessment might be to say, "This project is coming apart at the seams!" To which the sacred self replies, "So it seems." I've learned there's much going on that we do not see! Surrendering brings in all the resources available.

➤ Remember that no matter how difficult the circumstances, you are still the one having the experience, the one who can sit back and watch it all happening and give names to what is seen and felt. This makes you separate from and stronger than the experience.

➤ In quieter moments, ask for assistance finding the part of you which is unafraid. Expect a response.

➤ Release difficult circumstances to God, as you understand Him. Keep notes about what transpires.

CHAPTER 5
What to do when there is *No End In Sight:*

➤ Stop looking for an end. If it hasn't happened it is not real yet! Take comfort in this.

➤ Know with certainty that you're not seeing the future but only your imagination of what it might be.

➤ Start looking at your present reality. Today, this moment, right now, your actual life, the one happening right now, where you are? Are you safe now? Do you have food and warmth? Are those you care for safe and healthy? Do you have money now for what you need now, this afternoon? Can you draw a deep breath now? Are there things to be thankful for today? What are they?

➤ Express your gratefulness for this moment, for your breath, clothing, food and other items so basic to your survival that you take them for granted. Gratefulness matters. It changes *you* and a different you may be able to change other things.

➤ Choose a day or portion of a day and do something that

brings you joy. See this as a way to make a statement about the future you desire: I will no longer delay my joy, freedom and peace until conditions are right . . . I choose these qualities now.

➤ Again, surrender or release all views of the future: all that you fear has been lost and all you fear the future will bring you. Invite the universe into the very midst of the catastrophe.

➤ Keep a journal or notes of what happens.

CHAPTER 6
What to do when there is *No Escape:*

➤ When all paths of escape are blocked, assume it is time to stand still.

➤ Stop running, hiding, blaming others and making excuses.

➤ Stop the activity and busyness.

➤ Find moments in which to quietly breathe, open yourself now to receive a response from your sacred self (not your scared self), the one who has been with you from the beginning.

➤ Know that you are strong and courageous for ceasing much of your activity to turn and face yourself in this moment. Few people do this, choosing instead to stay busy. This response draws a powerful response from the universe.

➤ Continue the active work of being compassionate and patient with yourself even though this action seems irrelevant.

➤ As always, surrender all concerns and doubts.

➤ Practice gratitude; build into your days quiet moments for offering thanks.

➤ Continue keeping notes of what happens when you

surrender something to spirit. Remember, you are building credible evidence of a different, more powerful way of living.

CHAPTER 7
What to do when the *imaginary self* begins to crumble:

➤ Know with certainty this time will have an end. Sometimes you can only stand back and watch your life do what it needs to do; this is one of those times.
➤ Summon the courage to step back, stand down from your life, and rest.
➤ Using whatever amount of faith you have, surrender all concerns to Spirit.
➤ Know, with certainty, you've been heard. Look for nothing, expect nothing other than you have made contact with the sacred. Remember, there is more to who you are than the forceful or cautious part; the true you which lies waiting is much stronger, more balanced, and capable of great things—none of which may be visible from your current vantage point.
➤ Practice acknowledging out loud and then laying aside the societal messages you were given which served you in the past and kept you safe and alive; they may not serve you now. Remember, these old maps should have a "use by____" date stamped on them but we seldom pay attention! They're outdated. Lay them aside.
➤ Avoid excesses in alcohol, drugs, sex and activity that seem to have no purpose other than keeping you distracted. Some days you need a distraction; the issue here is excess.
➤ Do something fun that the old you would never ordinarily do.

What to do when the *figurine god* disappears:

> ➤ Do not trust and act upon only what you see and hear physically; find ways to quiet yourself by walking, running, or sitting so you can hear your body's wisdom or knowing.
>
> ➤ Stop analyzing and evaluating the deeper current of your life. It runs on a different time, pace, and schedule. It is always right even though you may feel it is too late or premature. Step into and experience each day without understanding or knowing why.
>
> ➤ Remember that every day, every experience, is sacred, especially the moment *after* surrender. You may feel like nothing is happening in your life and that you're going nowhere, but nothing is wasted by the universe. Old parts of you are dying now; you're likely to feel down, confused, bored or lost. Accept that feeling this way is okay and then choose to do something you enjoy.
>
> ➤ Surrender. Each day, many times a day if needed, allow the weight of worry to slip from your shoulders.
>
> ➤ Get quiet. Breathe deeply. Relax into the present moment. You can be clear about the results you desire without knowing how or where to begin. Find what your real intention is now (receiving) and entrust into the hands of the sacred what you cannot control (giving).

What to do when our *external signposts* disappear:

> ➤ Avoid excesses in alcohol, drugs, sex, work, inane activity, and other addictions. This is a significant time of realignment down to the cellular level. Be present for it!
>
> ➤ Feel the weight and value you have assigned to the societal standards from which you are breaking free.

For most of us they are based upon fear; below the fear you will find anger, and below the anger, sadness. Get in touch with the sadness—what does it say to you? Hint: somewhere along the line, you stopped playing your own unique tune.

➤ Ask yourself if these external standards define your true essence, the "all of me" that defies any box you might put around it. Do not give yourself away to standards which exist outside of yourself. They are too small for you!

➤ Cultivate silence, attentiveness, and relationships to key people in your life. Find a balance between healthy solitude and unhealthy isolation.

➤ Get in touch with nature, which continues on its intended way regardless of small crises we experience. The "nature" of nature shows us how we should relate to interim places: this period of your life, too, will pass. Go on your way and experience everything, but hold on to nothing.

➤ Recognize that old definitions of yourself are passing away and that you are grieving the loss. Grief seldom shows up in a nicely wrapped package that says, "Grief, please handle with care." You may instead feel ugly, worthless, and quite useless. Give your grief to the sacred and you will receive new and greater life back. Trust me on this.

CHAPTER 8
Ways to continue opening and trusting your heart:

➤ Be gentle with yourself during this time of transformation; you will see many aspects of yourself which may shock, embarrass and confuse you. Suspend judgment as best as you can. Your entire repertoire of competencies is being deepened and expanded.

➤ Stop all comparisons between you and others today. Right now. Comparisons create suffering. The life you live is unique from all others. Live it like nothing else matters.

➤ You're outgrowing the small boxes in which you've kept your gender identity. You can still be a good man even when you allow things to happen by being at the helm-driving action. You can still be a real woman when you're in charge, directing action or doing other things for yourself.

➤ Do little things each day that bring you joy. This is a demanding discipline and a skill worthy of development.

➤ Make one contact with and observation of nature each day: Yesterday, a mourning dove sat just over my shoulder on the telephone wire and sang her song; I felt lonely and called my brother. Keep an awareness of the larger community around you. Appreciate its beauty.

➤ Find a moment for expressing your gratitude on a regular basis.

CHAPTER 9
What to do to claim your true power and voice:

➤ You need only walk through what you fear! But walk through like you have been learning to do through this whole time of change.

➤ Acknowledge your experience . . . your feelings . . . the impossible sense of it all . . .

➤ Release these feelings and assessments (because, after all, they are just your assessments of what you can see; not the whole story) . . .

➤ Surrender yourself and the circumstances to the sacred . . .

- ➤ Stage small experiments where you can practice new behaviors.
- ➤ Pay attention, be vigilant but not obsessed . . .
- ➤ Go about your day and do what is in you to do today.
- ➤ Be gentle with yourself and know you are not alone.
- ➤ See this as a time for your transformation even if you're terrified and want none of it. Ask what you need to see or learn.
- ➤ You don't have to do this time flawlessly; commit to being present to what happens.
- ➤ You don't have to undo or make up in one day what took you years to develop. Be patient yet open your mouth and speak about what you know. Trust your inner voice to know when and what to do or say.
- ➤ Remember, you have stood and faced terrifying things during this period. Your capacity for courage, for landing on your feet is much greater than you may realize.

CHAPTER 10
What to do to remain unattached to what you desire:

- ➤ Be especially mindful of those desires that feel urgent and bring you impatience and fear. Ask, "What do I need to learn or see here?"
- ➤ Notice times when you feel very excited and good about yourself following successful outcomes and how especially low, even despondent you might feel following setbacks. You're continuing to identify with external events in ways that may not be helpful. No judgment here; just pay attention to what happens in you.
- ➤ Conversely, notice how inwardly steady you've become, how anchored and sure, when your heart has shifted from "I'm good because" . . . to "I'm good, period." Rejoice here!
- ➤ Distinguish, wherever possible, the difference

between what you want and how to get there. We easily become attached to our viewpoints and opinions about how to move forward. If we don't immediately know how, they become small boxes that trap us and hurt others.

➤ More time, money, personal time, more freedom and autonomy all feel like end results but instead are steps to something else. What would you do with more time . . . money . . . autonomy, etc.? When you feel delayed or obstructed, kept from what you want, sometimes you're meant to stop and get clear about what matters.

➤ There are, in fact, important things that need to happen within certain timeframes, budgets, etc. Get clear what these end results are as quickly as possible and commit the steps, the doing them, the "how to" to your sacred partners.

➤ Pay close attention to those things that bring you joy, that simply bring spontaneous pleasure to you. Notice any patterns: where are you, what are you doing, how are you being and with whom are you doing and being these things when you feel most alive? Do and invite into your life more of these!

➤ Invent ways and time to be present to the natural world. Take a walk, sit on your porch, listen to the world immediately around you. Watch the ways in which other beings work. The sparrows, wind and summer rain, the creek on the other side of town. Don't think too hard; rather, relax and focus. Ask your sacred partner: "What can I learn here?"

CHAPTER 11
How to walk in the new partnership with spirit and your sacred self:

➤ Give your spoken intention for this partnership to continue being made more real, visible and active in your life.

➤ Find a way to create a sacred ritual to celebrate your decision for partnership. Acknowledge all of the events that brought you to this moment, speak of what you've learned and what you've struggled with. Turn and face this moment and call in the assistance, comfort and companionship from your sacred partners that you need.

➤ Pay special attention to times when you're upset and feeling a need to do something. Ask, 'Does this serve my fear or my essence?' then decide what to do.

➤ Gratitude, balancing activity with solitude, doing things that bring you joy. You know the routine by now.

➤ Surrender. Each day invite spirit in to all aspects of your life and into the lives of those with whom you share important connection. Continue watching and recording what happens.

CHAPTER 12
Standing in the Fire Without Getting Burned; Notes for Those Who Would Help

NOTES FOR LEADERS AT WORK

➤ Above all else, work on yourself.

➤ Pay attention to the present. There is much you do not see and cannot know about without compassionate inquiry.

➤ Engage people where they are before demanding that they move.

➤ Release your concerns about circumstances and people to your higher power.

## NOTES FOR LEADERS AT HOME

➤ Remember, our work as helpers is not to do things but to be things for others.
➤ Decide: whose problem is it?
➤ Be clear about your boundaries.
➤ Release with love those circumstances and people you are concerned about.
➤ Surrender quickly, consistently, and often.
➤ Notice how controlling you are even when surrendering!
➤ Find ways to take care of and nurture yourself.
➤ Cultivate a stance of gratefulness.

# BIBLIOGRAPHY

Barks, Coleman Trans. *The Essential Rumi*. Harper San Francisco, 1995.

Bennis, Warren. *On Becoming a Leader*. Addison-Wesley, 1989.

Blake, William. *William Blake* (The Oxford Authors), ed. Michael Mason. Oxford University Press, 1988.

Block, Peter. *Stewardship: Choosing Service Over Self Interest*. Barrett-Koehler, 1993.

Block, Peter. *The Answer To How Is Yes: Acting On What Matters*. Barrett-Koehler, 2002.

Bly, Robert. Editor. *News of the Universe: Poems of Twofold Consciousness*. Sierra Club Books, 1980.

Bly, Robert. Translator. *Selected Poems of Rainier Maria Rilke*. Harper & Row Publishers, 1981.

Blum, Ralph. *The Book of Runes: Handbook for the Use of the Ancient Oracle*. St. Martin's Press, 1993.

Chodrön, Pema. *Start Where You Are: A Guide to Compassionate Living*. Shambala Publishers, 1994.

Chodrön, Pema. *The Wisdom of No Escape*. Shambala Publishers, 1991.

Cooper, Robert and Sawak, Ayman. *Executive EQ: Emotional Intelligence in Leadership and Organizations*. Grosset/Putnam, 1996.

Dreamer, Oriah Mountain. *The Invitation*. Harper San Francisco, 1999.

Hall, Brian. *Values Shift: A Guide to Personal and Organizational Transformation*. Twin Lights Publishing, 1994.

Hillman, James. *The Soul's Code: In Search of Character and Calling*. Random House, 1996.

Hudson, Frederick. *The Adult Years*. Jossey-Bass, 1991.

Jaworski, Jerry. *Synchronicity*. Berrett-Koehler Publishers, 1996.

Kaplan, Robert. *Beyond Ambition*. Jossey-Bass, 1991.
Kegan, Robert. *In Over Our Heads*. Harvard University Press, 1994.
Leggett, Trevor. *Zen and the Ways*. ("The New Flute" is attributed here.) Shambala Publishers, 1978.
Ladinski, Daniel. *The Gift: Poems by Hafiz, The Great Sufi Master*. Penguin Arkana, 1999.
Mitchell, Stephen. Editor. *The Enlightened Heart*. Harper & Row Publishers, 1989.
Mitchell, Stephen. Editor and Translator. *The Selected Poetry of Rainier Maria Rilke*. Vintage International, a division of Random House, 1989.
Morgan, Marlo. *Mutant Message Down Under*. HarperCollins, 1991
Moyne, John and Barks, Coleman. *Open Secret Versions of Rumi*. Threshold Books, 1984.
Nachmanovitch, Stephen. *Free Play: Improvisation in Life and Art*. Jeremy P. Tarcher/Putnam, 1990.
Noer, David M. *Healing the Wounds: Overcoming the Trauma of Layoffs and Revitalizing Downsized Organizations*. Jossey-Bass Management, 1993.
Oliver, Mary. *Dream Work*. Atlantic Monthly Press Publishers, 1986.
Senge, Peter. *The Fifth Discipline*. Currency Doubleday, 1990.
Somé, Malidoma Patrice. *Ritual: Power, Healing, and Community*. Penguin Arkana, 1993.
Apol, Laura and Watson, Jerry. Editors. *Learning to Live in The World: Earth Poems by William Stafford*. Harcourt, Brace & Company, 1994.
Styron, William. *Darkness Visible: A Memoir of Madness*. Vintage Books, a division of Random House, 1992.
Wheatley, Margaret. *Leadership and the New Science: Learning About Organization from an Orderly Universe*. Barrett-Koehler, 1992.

Whyte, David. *Songs for Coming Home*. Many Rivers
Press, 1989.

Wilson-Schaef, Anne. *Beyond Therapy, Beyond Science: A
New Model for Healing the Whole Person*.
HarperCollins, 1992.

Wright, Machelle Small. *MAP: The Co-Creative White
Brotherhood Medical Assistance Program*. Perelandra
Ltd, 1990.

# Engage Dan Holden for Seminars, Workshops, Retreats & More

Dan Holden is a master at transforming adversity into power, whether in personal or business situations. He is available to apply his extensive knowledge and experience with leaders in a variety of formats including retreats, workshops, seminars, talks and one-on-one coaching.

His work in the corporate world is unexcelled, and he is establishing a similarly outstanding reputation in the field of personal and spiritual growth. His "Bridges" series of workshops held in retreat are particularly powerful for mid to senior level executives and people in influential positions. They are transformational experiences the results of which are immediately applicable in participants' personal and professional lives.

To learn more about Dan Holden's work and the opportunities he offers, contact:

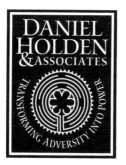

**dan@danielholdenassociates.com**

Or visit his website at:
**www.danielholdenassociates.com**

**Telephone 860-983-8203**

# I'd Like to Hear from You

We each have our share of hardship. Not everyone grapples with challenges and uses them for expanding awareness.

I've been fortunate enough to find a way to use my life as a laboratory in which to experiment, learn and prosper. Some of this I did on my own, while much of my learning has been shown to me by the Sacred. Maybe you've had a similar experience with Spirit (or whatever language you use) as a result of what I've put forth here.

If so, I invite you to share your experience and learning with me, so, with your permission, we might share them with others.

Send your experiences to:
**www.danielholdenassociates.com**

Don't worry about the form—we're most interested in the content.

Thanks,

Dan

www.wingfirepress.com

# O R D E R   F O R M

**WINGFIRE PRESS**
1028 Boulevard, #299
West Hartford, CT 06119-1801

WINGFIRE
PRESS

PLEASE SEND ME THE FOLLOWING:

| QUAN. | ITEM | PRICE |
|---|---|---|
| _____ | *Lost Between Lives* / Paperback $16.95 ea | _____ |
| | (CT residents add 6% Sales Tax) SALES TAX | _____ |
| | ($3.50 for first book, then $.50 for each add'l book) | |
| | SHIPPING | _____ |
| | TOTAL | _____ |

_____
NAME

_____
COMPANY NAME

_____
ADDRESS

_____
MAILING ADDRESS *(IF DIFFERENT FROM ABOVE)*

_____
CITY          STATE          ZIP

_____
HOME TELEPHONE          FAX          EMAIL

PAYMENT:

❑  Checks payable to *Wingfire Press* and mail to:
    1028 Boulevard, #299, West Hartford, CT 06119-1801

❑ VISA  ❑ MasterCard  ❑ AMEX  ❑ Discover

Cardnumber:_____

Name on card:_____

Exp. Date: _____ (mo) _____(year)

▪ Toll free order phone 800-431-1579 (secure message machine).
  Give mailing/shipping address, telephone number, MC/Visa
  name & card number plus expiration date.
▪ Secure Fax orders: 707-281-0851. Fill out this form & fax.
▪ On-line orders: www.wingfirepress.com
  orders@wingfirepress.com

www.wingfirepress.com

WINGFIRE PRESS
1028 Boulevard, #299
West Hartford, CT 06119-1801

WINGFIRE
PRESS

PLEASE SEND ME THE FOLLOWING:

| QUAN. | ITEM | PRICE |
|-------|------|-------|
| _____ | *Lost Between Lives* / Paperback $16.95 ea | _____ |
| | (CT residents add 6% Sales Tax) SALES TAX | _____ |
| | ($3.50 for first book, then $.50 for each add'l book) | |
| | SHIPPING | _____ |
| | TOTAL | _____ |

NAME

COMPANY NAME

ADDRESS

MAILING ADDRESS *(IF DIFFERENT FROM ABOVE)*

CITY          STATE       ZIP

HOME TELEPHONE       FAX       EMAIL

PAYMENT:

❑  Checks payable to *Wingfire Press* and mail to:
    1028 Boulevard, #299, West Hartford, CT 06119-1801

❑ VISA  ❑ MasterCard  ❑ AMEX  ❑ Discover

Cardnumber:_____

Name on card:_____

Exp. Date: _____ (mo) _____(year)

■ Toll free order phone 800-431-1579 (secure message machine).
  Give mailing/shipping address, telephone number, MC/Visa
  name & card number plus expiration date.
■ Secure Fax orders: 707-281-0851. Fill out this form & fax.
■ On-line orders: www.wingfirepress.com
  orders@wingfirepress.com

www.wingfirepress.com